Tai Ji Quan

Chen Kung Series

From the Private Family Records of Master Yang Luchan

Volume Three

Tai Ji Quan

太 極 拳

105-Posture Yang Style Solo Form
Instructions and Applications

by Chen Kung

Translation and Commentary
by Stuart Alve Olson

Valley Spirit Arts
Phoenix, Arizona

Translations from *Tai Ji Quan, Sword, Saber, Staff, and Dispersing Hands Combined* by Chen Kung (太極拳刀劍桿散手合綸, 陳公著, *Tai Ji Quan Dao Jian Gan San Shou He Lun, Chen Gong Zhe*).

Disclaimer

Please note that the author and publisher of this book are NOT RESPONSIBLE in any manner whatsoever for any injury that may result from practicing the techniques and/or following the instructions given within. Since the physical activities described herein may be too strenuous in nature for some readers to engage in safely, it is advised that a physician be consulted before training.

Library of Congress Control Number: 2017946004
ISBN-13: 978-1-5481-0537-2
ISBN-10: 1-5481-0537-6

Valley Spirit Arts, LLC
Series Editor: Patrick Gross
www.valleyspiritarts.com
contact@valleyspiritarts.com

In loving memory of Taijiquan Master
T.T. Liang
梁東材太極拳師
(1900 to 2002)

First and foremost, I wish to deeply thank Master Liang for not only encouraging me to translate Chen Kung's book, but for his sharing of so much knowledge. This series could not exist without having had his support.

Many thanks to all those who so generously contributed to our GoFundMe project so this book could be published. I sincerely bow to each and every one of you.

Thank you to Patrick Gross for editing and typesetting the books and producing the DVDs in the Chen Kung Series.

Lastly, I must express my gratitude to Vern Petersen, who long ago not only introduced me to Master Liang, but who was so supportive in the early stages of my translating of the Chen Kung Series.

**The Immortal Ancestor Zhang Sanfeng
Founder of Taijiquan**

A statue in his honor at Wu-Dang Temple,
Wu-Dang Mountain, Hubei Province, China.

Yang Family Lineage

Yang Style Founder, Yang Luchan
陽露禪
(1799–1872)

Yang Banhou
陽班侯
(1837–1892)
Son of Yang Luchan

Yang Jianhou
陽健侯
(1842–1917)
Son of Yang Luchan

Yang Shaohou
陽少侯
(1862–1930)
Son of Jianhou

Yang Chengfu
陽澄甫
(1883–1936)
Son of Jianhou

Contents

Zhang Sanfeng

Song Dynasty Immortal Ancestor and Founder of Taijiquan

Painting of Zhang Sanfeng watching a bird attacking a snake from his meditation hut on Wu-Dang Mountain, Hubei Province.

From the simple event of watching a bird attacking a snake, Master Zhang formulated the basic premises for the practice of Taijiquan.

As the snake evaded the strikes of the bird's beak and wings, Master Zhang noticed that it would coil and twist away when attacked. When the bird struck the snake's tail, the snake's head would immediately respond. If the bird then attacked the head, the snake's tail would respond. And when the bird resorted to assaulting the snake's body, its head and tail both responded.

After several failed attempts to defeat the snake, the bird surrendered and flew away.

From observing the snake, Zhang concluded that employing the entire body as one unit was more powerful than just moving the arms or legs independently, being pliable and relaxed meant greater efficiency and endurance of movement, and that the yielding can overcome the unyielding.

From the insights acquired in watching the bird and snake, Zhang was inspired to create the Thirteen Postures of Taijiquan.

Zhang Sanfeng is also credited with writing the *Tai Ji Quan Treatise* (太極拳論, *Tai Ji Quan Lun*)[1] and *Tai Ji Secret Arts of Refining the Elixir of Immortality* (太極煉丹秘訣, *Tai Ji Lian Dan Bi Jue*).[2] This later book is one of the best Internal Alchemy works in Chinese, wherein his meditation methods are especially effective and adaptable to modern culture.

1. See *Tai Ji Quan Treatise: Attributed to the Song Dynasty Daoist Priest Zhang Sanfeng* (Valley Spirit Arts, 2011) for a fuller biography of Zhang Sanfeng and a translation of this text.

2. See *Refining the Elixir: The Internal Alchemy Teachings of Daoist Immortal Zhang Sanfeng* (Valley Spirit Arts, 2014).

Biography of Master Chen Kung

Born in 1906, Master Chen Kung (a.k.a., Yearning K. Chen and Chen Yen-lin) passed away in Shanghai, China, in 1980. His book *Tai Ji Quan Sword, Saber, Staff, and Dispersing Hands Combined* revolutionized many aspects of Taijiquan practice and theory, especially those concerning his discourses on Intrinsic Energy (勁, Jin), Sensing Hands (推手, Tui Shou), Greater Rolling-Back (大攦, Da Lu), and Dispersing Hands (散手, San Shou). His explanations of intrinsic energies had never before appeared in any previous Taijiquan-related book, which really made him and his work an enigma.

In 1978, Master Jou Tsung-hwa met with him in Shanghai and reported that Chen started practicing Taijiquan at age four and was a doctor of Chinese medicine.

Around 1930, Chen Kung, a rich merchant and student of Yang Chengfu (陽澄甫) asked to borrow the family transcripts for just one evening so that he might read them to enhance his practice. Chen had been a loyal and dedicated student, so Yang Chengfu consented, knowing that in one night it would be difficult for even a fast reader to finish the book. What Yang didn't know was that Chen had hired seven transcribers to work through the night to copy the entire work. After Chen's disappearance (around 1932) he changed professions from merchant to doctor of Chinese medicine. During that year portions of the manuscript started appearing in various journals, which infuriated the Yang family.

Later, in 1943, Chen's entire copied notes appeared in book form and enjoyed rapid sales throughout China. This further infuriated the Yang family, who then released their own book claiming that Chen's publication was a forgery and that their new, smaller work was the genuine material. Chen, in typical Chinese fashion, claimed his book contained his own theories and that he only used the Yang family name for authenticity. This was Chinese politics at its best.

Master Liang told me this story. He had heard it through his teacher Prof. Cheng Man-ch'ing who heard it from his teacher, Yang Chengfu. With this kind of oral testimony I was never sure about the details. However, Master Jou Tsung-hwa said that Chen Kung confirmed the story when they met in 1978, and in 2005 Chen Kung's grandson, Donald Chen, confirmed it to me as well.

Before anyone accuses Chen Kung of any wrongdoing, clearly the Taijiquan world owes him a great debt, whatever the ethics or politics that were involved. The Yang family teachings might well have remained hidden or become lost; likewise, the Yang family might never have published the various works of their own. An even greater result was that many masters, for whatever reasons, began publishing their works as well. Chen's courage created a chain reaction of teachers going public with their knowledge.

In 1947, Chen Kung's *Tai Chi Ch'uan: Its Effects and Practical Applications* appeared from Willow Pattern Press in Shanghai, China. The book lists Yearning K. Chen as the author and Kuo Shuichang as the translator. The interesting thing about this book is that it doesn't appear to be wholly derived from the original 1943 Chinese version of Chen Kung's work used with my present translation. The chapters on physics, psychology, and morality included in the English edition make it completely distinct from the text I used for the series. The solo form instructions and practical application explanations are similar to the 1943 Chinese text, but the two are not identical by any other means, and it did not include the discourses on intrinsic energies[1] as presented in *Tai Ji Jin*.[2]

---

[1]   See note 9, p. 23.

[2]   *Tai Ji Jin: Discourses on Intrinsic Energies for Mastery of Self-Defense Skills* (vol. 2, Chen Kung Series) provides a full list with explanations of each intrinsic energy trained through Taijiquan practices. The information contained within this volume is unquestionably some of the most valuable and rare writings on Taijiquan.

Translator's Introduction

This particular volume in the Chen Kung Series represents the very core of the series because all the other volumes are based on the workings and principles of the 105-Posture Tai Ji Quan form detailed in this work.

In 1979, a book titled *Tai-Chi Ch'uan: The Effects & Practical Applications* by Chen Kung (translated and annotated by C. C. Chiu) was published by Newcastle Publishing Co., Inc. That book also presents a translation of Chen Kung's Taijiquan writings, but it lists 108 postures rather than the 105 in Chen Kung's original work. Even though this earlier work is a solid translation, it omits some very important elements from Chen Kung's work, such as the descriptions of the self-defense applications pertaining to each posture, references to the intrinsic energies used and developed in the posture movements, and the translations of the Chinese text within the posture illustrations.

Also, as anyone who has reviewed that work will attest, the English used is rather archaic and often difficult to understand. I have ensured that all the missing elements have been included in this work, and, I feel, are presented in a much clearer manner.

In the Appendix, I've added two key supplementary materials from my book *Tai Ji Quan Treatise: Attributed to the Song Dynasty Daoist Priest Zhang Sanfeng.* The first excerpt details the particulars of the vital Taijiquan principle of "calmly stimulating the Qi," which is the actual purpose behind Taijiquan practice. The second excerpt presents Chen Kung's list of the twenty-two *Foundational Principles of Tai Ji Quan,* which are crucial to all Taijiquan forms and exercises.

Lastly, I hope this book serves the Taijiquan community well and adds to the collection of authoritative Taijiquan literature. As Master Liang always liked to say, "Chen Kung's work is the Bible of Taijiquan." After having now translated the bulk of Chen's work, I most definitely agree.

—Stuart Alve Olson
Spring, 2017

Tai Ji Quan

太

極

拳

by Chen Kung

十 三 勢 解

Shi San Shi Jie

The Thirteen Operations are sometimes considered to be thirteen different types of postures, but this truly is wrong. The Thirteen Operations are the Eight Gates [八門, Ba Men] and Five Activities [五行, Wu Xing]. The Eight Gates are the four straight directions and four diagonal directions.

The four straight directions are Warding-Off, Rolling-Back, Pressing, and Pushing. The four diagonal directions are Pulling, Splitting, Elbowing, and Shouldering. These then are directions of the Eight Gates and the arrangement of Yin and Yang being upside down so they rotate and return to their origin. Wherever these occur there is activity causing the body to be divided into steps, and there are then the Five Activities that support these eight points of the compass.

Of the Five Activities, Fire is Advance Step [進步, Jin Bu]; Water is Withdraw Step [退步, Tui Bu]; Wood is Look Left [左顧, Zuo Gu]; Metal is Gaze Right [右盼, You Pan]; and Earth is Central Equilibrium [中定, Zhong Ding], because Central Equilibrium is the central pivot upon which all the others work. These, then, are the first principles of the Thirteen Operations.

From them come the styles of Thirteen Operations Boxing [十三勢拳, Shi San Shi Quan], which also correspond to Long

Boxing [長拳, Zhang Quan]. Because in former times the training of Tai Ji Quan meant starting by engaging in each of the individual styles until becoming experienced and proficient with them through repetitive training of each style. Lest over time it would be easy to become unctuous or perhaps enter into the hard styles of boxing.

There is no one fixed way of boxing, but in the end all the styles are true to their particular training of proficiency and skills. Together they connect and are coherent with each other, coming together as one framework, and unceasingly flow together and revolve back to their origin.

The names [of the Thirteen Postures] are used in Long Boxing. Long Boxing is Thirteen Posture Boxing, and so the names are likewise used in Tai Ji Quan, but they can be distinguished separately as Long Boxing. So people presently separated them and erroneously say there is only one form of Long Boxing. Afterwards others wrote books about this, but they did not have the proper transmissions.

The Designated Names of Tai Ji Quan (Long Boxing and Thirteen Postures)

太極拳 (即長拳亦 即十三勢拳) 名稱

Tai Ji Quan (Ji Zhang Quan Yi Ji Shi San Shi Quan) Ming Cheng

1) Beginning Tai Ji Quan Posture
太極拳起勢, Tai Ji Quan Qi Shi

2) Grasping the Sparrow's Tail (Right Style)
攬雀尾 (右式), Lan Qiao Wei (You Shi)

The image is of holding a bird, one hand on the breast and the other its tail.

3) Grasping the Sparrow's Tail (Left Style)
攬雀尾 (左式), Lan Qiao Wei (Zuo Shi)

4) Ward-Off
掤, Peng

The Chinese character used for Ward-Off (掤, Peng) cannot be found in the dictionaries as it is a made-up term used specifically in Yang Style Taijiquan. In older works, Peng translates as "to collide."

5) Roll-Back
攦, Lu

The Chinese character used for Roll-Back (攦, Lu) cannot be found in the dictionaries as it a made-up

3

term used specifically in Yang Style Taijiquan. In older works, Lu translates as "pull (or guide) back."

6) Press
擠, Ji
The energy comes from the hand attached to the forearm.

7) Push
按, An
The left hand guides and the right hand issues the energy.

8) Single Whip
單 鞭, Dan Bian
The idea is akin to the actions of a whip wherein the length of the whip is soft, but energy is issued at the very end like the cracking of a whip. Three actions in this posture are whip-like.

9) Lifting Hands Posture
提手上勢, Ti Shou Shang Shi
Makes use of Pulling energy where the opponent's wrist is pulled down as the elbow is raised upwards.

10) White Crane Cooling Its Wings
白鶴涼翅, Bai He Liang Chi
The hands of the opponent are separated, one up and one down, then a kick may be issued.

11) Brush the Knee and Twist Step (Left Style)
摟膝拗步 (左 式), Lou Xi Ao Bu (Zuo Shi)
Brushing is the action of clearing out a kick or punch.
Twist Step is either the turning in of the rear foot in which to provide the conditions for issuing energy from the

bottom of the foot, or an actual sliding of the foot forward when advancing into an opponent.

12) Hands Strum the Lute

手揮琵琶, Shou Hui Pi Pa

Alternately translated as *Playing the Guitar.* The Pi Pa is a four stringed instrument with twelve to twenty-six frets, dating back some two thousand years in Chinese history. Calling it a guitar is somewhat a misnomer, even though both are classified as plucked instruments. The instrument is normally held and played with the lower body of the instrument resting on the lap, the left hand extended out to work the frets and the right hand held back to pluck the strings, just like in the posture. Makes use of Splitting energy wherein the opponent's wrist is pushed to the left while the elbow is pushed to the right.

13) Brush the Knee and Twist Step (One)

摟膝拗步 (一), Lou Xi Ao Bu (Yi)

14) Brush the Knee and Twist Step (Two)

摟膝拗步 (二), Lou Xi Ao Bu (Er)

15) Brush the Knee and Twist Step (Three)

摟膝拗步 (三), Lou Xi Ao Bu (San)

16) Hands Strum the Lute

手揮琵琶, Shou Hui Pi Pa

17) Brush the Knee and Twist Step (Left Style)

摟膝拗步 (左 式), Lou Xi Ao Bu (Zuo Shi)

18) Swipe Across the Body and Chop

撇身捶, Pie Shen Chui

Swiping means to carry an opponent's arm to the downwards diagonal to cause them to fall off balance.

19) Step Forward, Remove, Parry, and Punch

進步搬攔捶, Jin Bu Ban Lan Chui

This is simply a means of taking an opponent off balance from their incoming strike. *Remove* and *Parry* are the functions of circling the opponent's arm around to execute a *Punch*.

20) Sealing to Appear As Closing

如封似閉, Ru Feng Si Bi

Usually this posture is translated as *Apparent Closure* or *Withdraw and Push*, but the meaning is deeper. First, an opponent's Push or strike is *Sealed* by carrying their lead arm back and downwards to the diagonal, and then the body can be pushed.

21) Embrace Tiger, Return to the Mountain

抱虎歸山, Bao Hu Gui Shan

The image is of carrying a tiger, but in application it is throwing an opponent off balance.

22) Ward-Off, Roll-Back, Press, and Push

掤攦擠按, Peng Lu Ji An

23) Diagonal Single Whip

斜單鞭, Xie Dan Bian

24) Punch Under Elbow

肘底捶, Zhou Di Chui

The *Punch* is potential, concealed beneath the elbow so the opponent cannot detect it.

25) Moving Backwards to Chase the Monkey Away (Right Style)

倒攆猴 (右式), Tao Nian Hou (You Shi)

In application, this posture is the opposite of *Brush Knee and Twist Step*. It is meant to draw the opponent back and into a Push.

26) Moving Backwards to Chase the Monkey Away (Left Style)

倒攆猴 (左式), Tao Nian Hou (Zuo Shi)

27) Diagonal Flying Posture

斜飛勢, Xie Fei Shi

Image is of an immortal taking flight. In application it is a movement of toppling an opponent via knocking them off balance with one foot behind their leg and your arm coming across their chest.

28) Lifting Hands Posture

提手上勢, Ti Shou Shang Shi

29) White Crane Cooling Its Wings

白鶴涼翅, Bai He Liang Chi

30) Brush the Knee and Twist Step (Left Style)

摟膝拗步 (左式), Lou Xi Ao Bu (Zuo Shi)

31) Needle at Sea Bottom

海底針, Hai Di Zhen

Image is of sticking one's hand in the water to retrieve a needle. In application, the movement brings an opponent down and off balance.

32) Fan Penetrates the Back

扇通背, Shan Tong Bei

The image is like the opening of a fan.

33) Turn Body, Swipe Across Body and Chop

轉身撇身捶, Zhuan Shen Pie Shen Chui

34) Step Forward, Remove, Parry, and Punch

進步搬攔捶, Jin Bu Ban Lan Chui

35) Step Forward to Ward-Off, Roll-Back, Press, and Push

上步掤攦擠按, Shang Bu Peng Lu Ji An

36) Single Whip

單鞭, Dan Bian

37) Cloud Hands

雲手, Yun Shou

An image of holding a cloud and moving it across the sky.

38) Single Whip

單鞭, Dan Bian

39) High Pat on Horse

高探馬, Gao Cai Ma

Image is of one hand under the horse's chin as the other hand strokes its head.

40) Separate Foot, Right

右分脚, You Fen Jiao

This type of kick is to the knee or shinbone, with the outer side of the foot making contact. For information on the Taijiquan kicks, see *Tai Ji Qi*, volume 1, under the section

"Cai Tui Exercise (Pulling Leg)." These exercises form the basis for all the Taijiquan kicking techniques.

41) Separate Foot, Left

左分脚, Zuo Fen Jiao

42) Turn Body and Kick With the Sole

轉身蹬脚, Zhuan Shen Deng Jiao

This kick makes use of the sole of the foot to make contact with the opponent.

43) Left and Right Brush Knee and Twist Step

左右摟膝拗步 (左式), Lou Xi Ao Bu

44) Advance Step to Plant Punch

進步栽捶, Jin Bu Zai Chui

The punch is directed into the opponent's thigh

45) Turn Body, Swipe Across Body and Chop

轉身撇身捶, Zhuan Shen Pie Shen Chui

46) Step Forward, Remove, Parry, and Punch

進步搬攔捶, Jin Bu Ban Lan Chui

47) Kick With Right Foot

右踢脚, You Ti Jiao

This is a toe kick jabbing technique.

48) Strike Tiger, Left

左打虎, Zuo Da Hu

Image is of the hands coming across to strike both sides of a tiger's head.

49) Strike Tiger, Right

右打虎, You Da Hu

50) Kick With Right Foot
右踢脚, You Ti Jiao
This is a toe kick jabbing technique.

51) Double Winds to Both Ears
雙風貫耳, Shuang Feng Guan Er
A strike to both ears of the opponent.

52) Kick With Left Foot
左踢脚, Zuo Ti Jiao
This is a toe kick jabbing technique.

53) Turn Body and Kick With the Sole
轉身蹬脚, Zhuan Shen Deng Jiao

54) Swipe Across the Body and Chop
撇身捶, Pei Shen Chui

55) Step Forward, Remove, Parry, and Punch
進步搬攔捶, Jin Bu Ban Lan Chui

56) Sealing As If to Appear As Closing
如封似閉, Ru Feng Si Bi

57) Embrace Tiger, Return to the Mountain
抱虎歸山, Bao Hu Gui Shan

58) Ward-Off, Roll-Back, Press, and Push
掤攦擠按, Peng Lu Ji An

59) Horizontal Single Whip
橫單鞭, Heng Dan Bian

60) Wild Horse Parting Its Mane (Right Style)
野馬分鬃 (右式), Ye Ma Fen Zong (You Shi)
Image is of two hands holding a horse's mane and separating it into two parts.

61) Wild Horse Parting Its Mane (Left Style)

野馬分鬃 (左 式), Ye Ma Fen Zong (Zuo Shi)

62) Wild Horse Parting Its Mane (Right Style)

野馬分鬃 (右 式), Ye Ma Fen Zong (You Shi)

63) Grasping the Sparrow's Tail (Left Style)

攬雀尾 (左 式), Lan Qiao Wei (Zuo Shi)

64) Step Forward to Ward-Off, Roll-Back, Press, and Push

上步掤攦擠按, Shang Bu Peng Lu Ji An

65) Single Whip

單鞭, Dan Bian

66) Jade Maiden Weaves at Shuttles (1)

玉女穿梭 (一), Yu Nu Chuan Suo (Yi)

Image is of a woman working a shuttle to make cloth, with one hand on the lower bar and the other on the upper.

67) Jade Maiden Weaves at Shuttles (2)

玉女穿梭 (二), Yu Nu Chuan Suo (Er)

68) Jade Maiden Weaves at Shuttles (3)

玉女穿梭 (三), Yu Nu Chuan Suo (San)

69) Jade Maiden Weaves at Shuttles (4)

玉女穿梭 (四), Yu Nu Chuan Suo (Si)

70) Grasping the Sparrow's Tail (Left Style)

攬雀尾 (左 式), Lan Qiao Wei (Zuo Shi)

71) Step Forward to Ward-Off, Roll-Back, Press, and Push

上步掤攦擠按, Shang Bu Peng Lu Ji An

72) Single Whip
單鞭, Dan Bian

73) Cloud Hands
雲手, Yun Shou

74) Single Whip
單鞭, Dan Bian

75) Snake Lowering Its Body
蛇身下勢, She Shen Xia Shi
Image is of a snake slithering down a boulder or tree to the ground.

76) Golden Rooster Stands on One Leg (Right Style)
金雞獨立 (右式), Jin Ji Tu Li (You Shi)
Image is of a *Golden Rooster*, or *Crane*, standing perfectly balanced on one leg.

77) Golden Rooster Stands on One Leg (Left Style)
金雞獨立 (左式), Jin Ji Tu Li (Zuo Shi)

78) Moving Backwards to Chase the Monkey Away
倒攆猴, Tao Nian Hou

79) Diagonal Flying Posture
斜飛勢, Xie Fei Shi

80) Lifting Hands Posture
提手上勢, Ti Shou Shang Shi

81) White Crane Cooling Its Wings
白鶴涼翅, Bai He Liang Chi

82) Brush the Knee and Twist Step
摟膝拗步, Lou Xi Ao Bu

83) Needle at Sea Bottom
海底針, Hai Di Zhen.

84) Fan Penetrates the Back
扇通背, Shan Tong Bei

85) Turn Body, White Snake Spits Out Tongue
轉身白蛇吐信, Zhuan Shen Bai She Tu Xin
Many forms have eliminated this action as it is the same as *Swipe Across the Body and Chop*, but here the chop is replaced with finger thrust to the opponent's throat, imagined as a snake spitting out its tongue.

86) Step Forward, Remove, Parry, and Punch
進步搬攔捶, Jin Bu Ban Lan Chui

87) Step Forward to Ward-Off, Roll-Back, Press, and Push
上步掤攦擠按, Shang Bu Peng Lu Ji An

88) Single Whip
單鞭, Dan Bian

89) Cloud Hands
雲手, Yun Shou

90) Single Whip
單鞭, Dan Bian

91) High Pat on Horse
高探馬, Gao Cai Ma

92) Crossing Hands
十字手, Shi Zi Shou

93) Turn Body to Cross Legs
轉身十字腿, Zhuan Shen Shi Zi Tui
This is kick with the sole technique.

94) Brush the Knee and Direct Punch to Groin
摟膝指襠捶, Lou Xi Zhi Dang Chui

95) Step Forward to Ward-Off, Roll-Back, Press, and Push
上步掤攦擠按, Shang Bu Peng Lu Ji An

96) Single Whip
單鞭, Dan Bian

97) Snake Lowering Its Body
蛇身下勢, She Shen Xia Shi

98) Step Forward to Seven Star
上步七星, Shang Bu Qi Xing
The *Seven Star* is actually the Big Dipper.

99) Retreat Step to Ride the Tiger
退步跨虎, Tui Bu Kua Hu
Image is that of withdrawing from an advancing tiger in order to mount its back.

100) Turn Body to Sweep the Lotus Blossoms
轉身擺蓮, Zhuan Shen Bai Lian
The feet move to clear away the lotus blossoms. This kicking action is a sweep of the opponent's front leg. The second kick is either directed to the opponent's kidney or to the back of their thigh.

101) Bend Bow to Shoot the Tiger

彎弓射虎, Wan Gong She Hu

The body is moved out and forward, and the arms move like drawing back a bowstring ready to shoot the tiger.

102) Swipe Across the Body and Chop

撇身捶, Pei Shen Chui

103) Step Forward, Remove, Parry, and Punch

進步搬攔捶, Jin Bu Ban Lan Chui

104) Sealing to Appear As Closing

如封似閉, Ru Feng Si Bi

105) Conclusion of Tai Ji

合太極, He Tai Ji

太極拳

Tai Ji Quan

1) Beginning Tai Ji Quan Posture[1]

太極拳起勢

Tai Ji Quan Qi Shi

此乃沉肩

肩不宜高
高曰寒肩

手指勿墜下墜下
則神不貫頂

（1）太極拳起勢

17

Fixed Standing Instructions

The feet are separated and on line with each other, with the
distance between them equal to that of the shoulders. The
hands are held flat [with the thumbs touching] against the sides
of the thighs, palms down, fingers pointing forward, and
without applying strenuous tension.[2] The elbows are kept
slightly bent.[3] The eyes gaze forward.[4] The tongue is held
against the upper palate.[5] The lips and teeth are [lightly] held
together.[6] Breathe through the nose.[7] Retain a light and
sensitive energy on top of the head.[8] Sink the shoulders and
suspend the elbows.[9] Hollow the chest and raise the back.[10]
Sink the Qi to the lower Elixir Field.[11] Be relaxed and open
so the entire body is loose, allowing Qi and blood to flow
freely throughout.[12] (See Illustration #1.)

Illustration #1 Text

Incorrect if the shoulders are high. High shoulders are called
    Poor (or Cold) Shoulders.
The hands are not to be collapsed down, collapsing them
    down results in the spirit from the top of the head not being
    able to be as if suspended by a thread. This is also called
    "sink the shoulders."

Active Movement Instructions

Without applying strength in the hands, slowly raise them
to the front until they are on line with the shoulders.
    Then bend the knees into a squatting position while
simultaneously bringing the back of the right hand to be
in front of the chest.

Raise the body and turn to the left. Angle the right hand to the right in front of the body, bringing the back of the left hand to the front of the chest. Turn both palms upward.

The right hand is then swiped[13] towards the left, swiping across until it draws near to the left hand, while the left hand turns downward (using the wrist), and the fingers of the left hand point downwards.

Move [both hands] in a level circle, and turning the left palm upwards again. Bring both hands so they are in front of the left ribs (left hand is below, and the right hand above). Do this as if embracing an object.

Then rotate both hands towards the right half of the body in front of the ribs, while swapping the upper and lower positions of the palms so they are opposite of each other. Using the wrist, the right palm moves downward towards the right, making a level half circle, while turning the right palm so it faces upwards, and the left palm is turned downwards (so the left hand is above, and right hand below).

Rotate both palms, returning them back to the left half of the body, in front of the left flank area (do not change the positions of the hands). Rotate the hands again to bring them to the front of the chest. Move them to the right and downwards, making two level half circles, one smaller than the other and one lower than the other, the lower one being the smaller. At the same time, while gradually bringing the body down into a squatting position, rotate the right hand to come beneath the left elbow (with the palm facing upward). The left-foot heel is then turned to the left.

Applications

The arms embody the mind-intent [意, Yi][14] of Ward-Off. The hands embody the mind-intent of Push. The shoulders are able to Shoulder, with the hips striking.

Chen Kung's Note

Every style of Tai Ji Quan can use these methods, which have a thousand changes and ten thousand transformations.[15] This document is intended to give practicers instructions that are easy to learn and use. Only simple methods are included and explained. While practicing, one should breathe through the nose to avoid dispersing of the spirit and bringing disorder to the Qi.[16]

Translator's Notes

1. The *Beginning Tai Ji Quan Posture* is divided into two parts of instruction: *Fixed Stance,* normally termed as Wu Ji (無極) and translated as the "Illimitable," denotes the condition before Yin and Yang separate and become Tai Ji. The second part, *Active Movement,* termed as Tai Ji (太極), is the condition when Yin and Yang separate, from which all Ten Thousand Things (萬物, Wan Wu, all phenomena) are brought into creation. In imagery, Wu Ji is an empty circle, and Tai Ji a circle that is halved by one side being white (Yang) and the other half being black (Yin).

2. *Strenuous tension* (呆力, Dai Li) would normally translate as "foolish or unneeded energy," which is actually the meaning of using strength and tension in Taijiquan. The opposite of this is *Song* (鬆) energy.

When people develop their intrinsic energy (see note 9), they reach a state of Song energy, which is akin to the energy of a cat (sensitive, alert, and relaxed). Normally, Song energy is translated into English as just "being completely relaxed," but it is much more than just that definition. With intrinsic energy comes a very heightened sense of alertness and sensitivity, so the "energy" being referred to is different from the internal energy of Qi. When the word "relax" appears in the text, think of and apply the ideas of Song energy, as this is the type of relaxation to which Chen Kung is referring.

3. *Keeping the elbows slightly bent* accomplishes two purposes: 1) This allows the blood and Qi to flow more freely, as locked joints create tension. 2) Keeping the elbows (and knees) slightly bent helps the body to relax and respond better to external conditions, such as an opponent's attack or an accidental fall. The image that best represents this principle is seen in toddlers who keep their joints slightly bent at all times.

4. *Eyes gazing forward* is not meant to mean an intense stare, but more in keeping with a spatial view, neither looking in nor out. Again, the perfect model for this are the bright eyes of infants.

5. *Curling up the tongue so that the tip connects to the upper palate* (上腭, Shang E) has two main purposes in Taijiquan practice. 1) This opens up the flow of saliva to keep the throat moist during practice and to help one breathe through the nose. 2) It maintains a connection between the Dumai Meridian (督脉,

along the spine) and the Renmai Meridian (任脈, on the front centerline of the body) so the Qi may flow freely through the mouth and into the front torso of the body. This point in the upper palate is sometimes called the Magpie Bridge (鵲橋, Que Qiao) or Heaven's Gate (天門, Tian Men).

6. *The lips and teeth held together* is done in a gentle manner, not with any tension whatsoever. Doing so prevents inhaling or exhaling through the mouth, which will create a dryness. Also, doing this correctly will take tension away from the entire facial area.

7. *Breathing through the nose* is called upon for three very important reasons: 1) Breathing through the mouth creates what Chinese medicine calls "fire in the throat," a dryness causing the breath to become erratic. 2) The nose, unlike the mouth, has hairs that filter debris from entering the lungs. 3) Breathing through the mouth does not allow the diaphragm membrane to function in its fullest capacity, whereas breathing through the nose allows this muscle to expand and contract more fully so that the breath can function more efficiently. See *Embryonic Breathing: The Taoist Method of Opening the Dan Tian* for more information on breathing for the development of Qi.

8. *Retain a light and sensitive energy on top of the head* (虛 領頂勁, Xu Ling Ding Jin) means to imagine there's a light, sensitive energy on top of the head, or to imagine that a thread is suspending the head from above. See *The Foundational Principles of Tai Ji Quan* in the Appendix.

9. *Sink the shoulders and suspend the elbows* (沉肩垂肘, Chen Jian Chui Zhou) is normally joined with the ideas of *seating the wrists* and *relaxing the fingers*. See *The Foundational Principles of Tai Ji Quan* in the Appendix. This entire principle is primarily employed to allow blood and Qi to flow through the entire arm and into the fingertips, as well as to create the conditions for intrinsic energy to be expressed out through the arms and hands.

   Intrinsic energy (勁, Jin) is the energy developed in the sinews and tendons through relaxed, sensitive, and alert use of employing the entire body as one unit. When a Taijiquan master pushes, for example, the opponent feels very little actual pushing strength coming from the master's hand. This is a result of the master's hands being sensitive, alert, and light, and not using any external muscular force. This doesn't mean the master is too soft and yielding to be in a state of collapse.

   Taijiquan is an external appearance of relaxation, but internally there is an alert vitality. In the case of *brute force* (拙力, Zhuo Li), it literally means "clumsy and unskilled strength." Taijiquan, however, makes use of both li (力, strength) and jin (勁, intrinsic energy).

   Probably the best analogy for this can be seen in how a gorilla uses its strength. It is surprising to see how relaxed a gorilla's muscles are when climbing or even fighting. Even though gorillas have great strength, they rarely express any muscular tension or strain in their movements.

10. *Hollow the chest and raise the back* (含胸拔背, Han Xiong Ba Bei) aids in the development of adhering Qi to the spine (raising the back) and sinking the Qi into the lower Elixir Field (hollowing the chest). But it also helps in keeping the back rounded out and sinking the shoulders so that there is no pinching of the shoulder blades together. See *The Foundational Principles of Tai Ji Quan* in the Appendix.

11. *Sink the Qi into the Elixir Field* (氣沉丹田, Qi Chen Dan Tian) has two important functions: 1) It keeps all the movements generating and functioning from the waist. 2) It keeps the mind-intention in the lower abdomen. See *The Foundational Principles of Tai Ji Quan* in the Appendix.

    Elixir Field (丹田, Dan Tian) refers to the area (or Qi center) located a few inches behind your navel, where the umbilical cord connects to the body. There are three Elixir Fields in the body—the Upper Elixir Field (between the eyes, or "Third Eye"), Middle Elixir Field (solar plexus), and Lower Elixir Field (behind the navel).

12. *Allow the blood and Qi to flow freely in the body* is another way of expressing the term *Free Circulation of Qi*. See the Appendix for an excerpt from *Tai Ji Quan Treatise* that provides an in-depth analysis of this important Taijiquan fundamental.

13. The term *swipe* (搨, Ta) comes from the Chinese character meaning "to rub," such as in rubbing the inscription from a stone engraving. Hence, the idea of swiping with the use of some energy.

14. *Mind-intent* (意, Yi), or will, is a reaction founded in awareness, intuition, and sensitive alertness. Mind-intent is "conditioned" in that it is developed over a long time from the practice of Taijiquan exercises. It is also "unconscious" in that the rational thinking mind is not used. The problem in defining mind-intent is an empirical one in that you must first be truly capable of sinking the Qi into the lower Elixir Field, which then strengthens the vitality of mind-intent, which in turn will affect the mind, producing tranquility. So without initiating the use of mind-intent, however vague at first, to sink the Qi into the lower Elixir Field, the mind-intent cannot be made strong enough for you to truly realize the difference between mind-intent and mind.

15. *A thousand changes and ten thousand transformations* (千變萬化, Qian Bian Wan Hua) is a term meaning an incalculable array of structure, application, and skills.

16. *Dispersing the spirit and bringing disorder to the Qi* (神散氣亂, Shen San Qi Luan) means that if the breath is not regulated, calm, and focused it will adversely affect the practitioner's state of mind and breath. The reason for this is that Taijiquan is a moving meditation relying on the body, breath, and mind to work as one unit.

2) Grasping the Sparrow's Tail (Right Style)
攬雀尾（右式）
Lan Qiao Wei (You Shi)

（式右）尾雀攬（２）

From the previous position, take a diagonal Advance Step [to the northeast] with the right foot. Separate the left and right hands simultaneously (the left hand moves downward, and the right hand moves upward). Shift the right hand and brachial area to the right side. It cannot be too straight or too far forward (with the right palm moving diagonally upward), bringing it to be on line with the chest. Move the left hand (palm facing downward) back to the left side, but not too far back. At the same time, bend the right knee, making a right diagonal Bow Stance.

The right foot is substantial and the left foot insubstantial. Rotate and take advantage of the power of the waist and thighs to the right side.

Relax the waist and coccyx. Bring the body downward into a slight squatting position, but not too far forward. When the head and body are correct, hollow the chest and raise the back. (See Illustration #2.) This is *Grasping the Sparrow's Tail (Right Style)*.

Illustration #2 Text
Suspend the head and keep the body upright.
Relax the waist and relax the coccyx.
Hold in the mind-intent of Warding-Off.
Do not let the [right] knee pass over the toes.

Applications
Grasp the opponent's left-hand wrist and step forward with the right foot. Your right hand attaches beneath the opponent's arm, and then your right flank can use horizontal intrinsic energy to Ward-Off to the opponent's chest and armpit area. But supposing your right hand is on the upper area of his hand and arm, then the object of Ward-Off should be to his arm and chest cavity.[1]

Translator's Note
1. See note under *Grasping the Bird's Tail (Left Style)* for further application instructions.

3) Grasping the Sparrow's Tail (Left Style)
攬雀尾（左式）

Lan Qiao Wei (Zuo Shi)

（式左）尾雀攬（3）

From the previous posture, turn the right hand downward. Follow this by bringing the waist and thighs to the left and back. As though grasping [攬, lan], the left hand should move to the left, from outside to inside. Then by circling around with the waist and thighs, rotate [the left hand] to be below the right elbow, and turning the palm upward. Shift the toes of the right foot horizontally to the right. Take an Advancing Diagonal Step with the left foot toward the left side [to the northwest]. Separate the left and right hands simultaneously. Advance to the left side with the left brachial area (the left palm is slanted upward), bringing it to be on line with the chest. Move the right hand to the right and back as though grasping. At the same time, bend the left knee and bring the body into a slight squatting position.

Seat the waist and relax the coccyx. Finish in a left diagonal Bow Stance. The left foot is substantial, and the right foot insubstantial. This posture is just like the right-side style. (See Illustration #3.) This is *Grasping the Sparrow's Tail (Left Style)*.

Illustration #3 Text
Suspend the head and keep the body upright.
Relax the waist and coccyx.
Keep to the mind-intent of Warding-Off.
Do not let the [left] knee pass over the toes.

Applications
Grasp the opponent's right-hand wrist and step forward with the left foot. The left hand attaches beneath the opponent's arm, and then your left flank can use horizontal intrinsic energy to Ward-Off to the opponent's chest and armpit area. But supposing your left hand is on the upper area of his hand and arm, then the object of Ward-Off should be to his arm or chest cavity.[1]

Translator's Note
1. In the first application the idea is to get beneath the opponent's incoming hand and arm, attaching to their

underarm and chest. Then from the rear leg issue horizontal intrinsic energy.

The second application also makes use of horizontal intrinsic energy but is done to the opponent's upper arm or to their chest cavity (solar plexus).

Even though the text here distinguishes between the right and left styles of *Grasping the Bird's Tail*, the applications can equally be used on either side.

4) Ward-Off

棚

Peng

棚 （ 4 ）

From the previous posture, turn the left palm downward, and while rotating the body to the right [north], circle the hand levelly in front of the chest. (At the same time, [the right hand] makes a small level circle beside the pelvic area.)

The body is to move into a squat, and both hands are centered between the knees. When squatting, make another small circle while rotating the right hand to move beneath the left elbow, and turning the palm upward. Turn and shift the toes of the left foot horizontally to the left. Take an Advancing Step with the right foot [east].

Bring the right hand and brachial area so they follow the waist and thighs when moving forward and upward into Ward-Off. Simultaneously, place the left hand on the inside of the right brachial area. Move forward to the right side until the brachial area is on line with the chest. At the same time, bend the left knee, bringing the body into a slight squat. The right side is substantial, and the left side insubstantial.

Retain a light and sensitive energy on top of the head. Hollow the chest and raise the back. Sink the shoulders and suspend the elbows. The Tail Gateway[1] is to be centered and upright. Adhere the Qi to the spine. The spirit of the eyes gazes forward. (See Illustration #4.)

Illustration #4 Text
Retain a light and sensitive energy on top of the head.
The spirit of the eyes gazes to the front.
The body should not lean forward.
The hands and arms are to be slightly bent and not held
    too high.
The [right] knee is not to extend beyond the toes.

Applications
Grasp the opponent's incoming hand, and then use both hands to form Ward-Off, or lean in to issue Ward-Off to the opponent's body.[2]

Translator's Note

1. *Tail Gateway* [尾閭, Wei Lu, tailbone area] is a gland and Qi center located about two and a half inches inside the anus on the upper part—not just on the tip of the tailbone as it's typically described. In Kundalini yoga this area is called the Kundalini gland.

    Keeping the Tail Gateway *centered and upright* aligns the spine and prevents leaning. To "draw in the Tail Gateway" means to tuck the tailbone in and down about one inch so there is no protrusion of the buttocks.

2. The first application is simply to Neutralize (化, Hua) the opponent's attack and the second application is to move into the opponent and issue out with Ward-Off.

5) Roll-Back

擺

Lu

擺 (5)

The left and right hands follow the movement of the waist and legs. Towards the front make a rightward circle [with the hands and arms], then bring them back to the left side while withdrawing and circling back. After withdrawing them back, the right palm is turned downward, and the left palm turned upward. Moving down and to the left rear, Rolling-Back.

The eyes gaze to the left side. Hollow the chest. Sink the shoulders. The left foot is substantial and the right foot insubstantial. (See Illustration #5.)

Do not squat down too far or be bent over. The intrinsic energy is like reeling silk[1] without severance.

Illustration #5 Text

If the intrinsic energy is too short it will not be easy to express. If going too long, the intrinsic energy will be easily interrupted.

Applications

From the previous application method of *Ward-Off*. Supposing your right hand [in Ward-Off] Opens [開, Kai] the opponent, and the opponent then changes by taking his left fist to strike your abdomen (or flank area). You should then Adhere [黏 貼, Zhan Tie] your right forearm to his left elbow. Simultaneously, taking your left hand to grasp and Pull the opponent's left wrist. Then moving towards the left side to Roll-Back, using the intrinsic energy of the waist and legs.

Translator's Note

1. *Reeling silk* [抽 絲, Chou Si] is a specialized Taijiquan term. In this reference it means the issuing of the intrinsic energy, jin, is to be performed by using the entire body as one unit with no interruption or stoppage within the movement. This is just like the idea of pulling silk from a cocoon, any stoppage will break the silk thread.

6) Press

擠

Ji

擠 (6)

At the time when the movement of *Roll-Back* is exhausted, the right-hand palm following along with a turning gesture [of the waist] is turned so the palm of the right hand faces toward the chest (held lower than with the Ward-Off posture). The left palm then adheres to the inside of the right forearm (the left hand and arm are more level than with the Ward-Off method). Following the movement of the waist and thighs, the two arms Press forward together, while the right knee bends to complete a Bow Stance. The right foot is substantial and the left foot insubstantial.

Sink the shoulders and suspend the elbows. Retain a light and sensitive energy on top of the head. Hollow the chest and raise the back. The spirit of the eyes gazes to the front. (See Illustration #6). The Tail Gateway is to be centered and upright. Sink the Qi into the lower Elixir Field.

Illustration #6 Text

If [the arms are] held too high the upper body will easily go
    beyond the point of being able to sink the shoulders.

Applications

Proceeding from the previous posture application method of *Roll-Back*, if the opponent moves downward, Pull and rotate his hand back. Bend your right knee, stretching out the waist and legs, and use the movement to Press towards the front with advancing forward. At this point use your intrinsic energy as though entering a bamboo stalk[1] by bringing the right forearm to face outwards and moving it upward and turning it out.

Translator's Note

1. *Entering a bamboo stalk* means there can be no wavering. Just like the Zen saying about a snake trying to get from one point to another, it has to make a lot of turning and coiling movements, but if it goes through a bamboo stalk it will get there directly.

7) Push
按
An

按 (7)

After *Press*, separate both hands towards the front. Following the movement of the waist and thighs, the left and right hands are circled as they move to the back to withdraw, sit in the left leg (bring both hands back in front of the chest. They should be several centimeters from the chest). The fingers are directed upward, with the palms facing forward. Hollow the chest, sink the shoulders, and suspend the elbows. The entire body is to be centered on the left leg.

Follow the waist and legs with an advancing movement to the front. Bend the right knee, and Push towards the front. The right foot changes and becomes substantial, and the left foot becomes insubstantial. (See Illustration #7.)

Retain a light and sensitive energy on top of the head. Hollow the chest and raise the back. Sink the shoulders and suspend the elbows. Seat the wrists and extend the fingers. Draw in the Tail Gateway. The spirit of the eyes follows the movement towards the front, gazing levelly. The upper body should not lean too far forward. The [right] knee should not extend over the toes.

Illustration #7 Text

If moving too far out the intrinsic energy will easily collapse.

Applications

1) From the previous application of *Press,* if downward pressure is put on your forearm by the opponent's hands, bring both your hands back and separate them, moving back to Neutralize [化, Hua] so the opponent falls on emptiness with his incoming movement. Afterwards his intrinsic energy will be severed. As soon as his energy is broken, Push both hands unto his chest cavity.

2) From the *Press* posture, if the opponent follows to the left side and returns with Press, you then take both his hands and raise them up so that he falls on emptiness with his incoming movement, then advance and Push with both hands.

8) Single Whip

單 鞭

Dan Bian

鞭 單 (8)

From the previous *Push* posture, both shoulders are sunk and the elbows suspended, bringing up to be on line with the upper chest, with both palms facing outward. Follow the momentum of the waist and legs by making a leftward turning movement.

At the same time, raise the right foot toes, and turn the foot towards the left. The weight should be entirely centered on the left leg. Afterwards shift [the weight] to the right leg. When the hands are circled back to be in front of the chest, suspend the five fingers of the right hand downward to create a Hooked Hand.[1] The left hand then moves down levelly to the center of the waist, with the palm turned upward, bringing it in alignment with the right hand with one above and the other below, as if holding a ball. Follow the momentum of the waist and legs by circling both hands to the right. Keeping the [weight on the right leg, raise the body and turn it leftward.

At the same time, raise the left foot and take a diagonal half-step to the left. From the right side of the chest, move the left hand from downward to upward, with the palm facing the interior. As it passes the face turn the palm to the left, keeping the palm open. Then turn the palm outward and move it forward and slightly downward.

At the same time, bring the body into a squatting position. Move with the momentum and shift [the weight] again to the left leg. Bend the left knee and slightly straighten the right leg, by leaving the knee slightly bent. The legs finish in a Bow Stance.

Relax the waist and relax the coccyx. The Tail Gateway should be centered and upright. The two arms are level and on line. Levelly sink the shoulders, and suspend the elbows, seat the wrists. Sink the Qi into the lower Elixir Field. The spirit of the eyes gazes forward and follows the left hand. (See Illustration #8.)

Illustration #8 Text

If [the Hooked Hand is] held too high the intrinsic energy will be lost.

If the knee is bent [rear leg] the center of balance will easily become too low to be seated.

Applications

1) If an opponent's left fist strikes the left side of your chest, use your left hand to Open [開, Kai] and separate by using Push to his left shoulder.

2) If the opponent's right fist strikes the right side of your chest, hook with your right hand and attack his chest with the back (or fist) of the right hand.

3) If an opponent strikes with the right hand, follow the momentum of the body and waist and simultaneously advance and strike with your palm to his armpit (or chest cavity).

Translator's Note

1. The *Hooked Hand* [勾手, Gou Shou] is formed by bringing together all five fingers. In application it is used for plucking, seizing, and striking vital Qi points. In some cases the back of the wrist of the Hooked Hand is used to strike vital points as well.

9) Lifting Hands Posture

提手上勢

Ti Shou Shang Shi

勢 上 手 提 (9)

From the previous *Single Whip* posture, raise the body and turn the left side [of the body] towards the right side. Return the center of balance to the left leg by following the momentum of shifting the toes of the left foot slightly to the right, and then shifting [the weight] to the left leg.

Raise the right foot. Take a half step forward. The heel of the foot should follow the ground. Raise the toes of the foot and bring the body into a squat and seat the waist. The hands are mutually moved to the interior and raised together, with the palms diagonally opposite of each other, with the right hand in front and the left hand behind.

Sink the shoulders and suspend the elbows. Hollow the chest and raise the back. Relax the waist and relax the coccyx. Draw in the Tail Gateway. The spirit of the eyes gazes to the front. The two arms are relaxed and open as initially in Ward-Off. Do not clamp [the hands] together. Do not draw the body up too high nor position it too low. (See Illustration #9.)

Illustration #9 Text
Sink the shoulders. Suspend the elbows downward.
The body is not to be held too high. If too high the intrinsic
    energy will be severed.

Applications
1) If an opponent's incoming strike is to your chest with his left hand, use your upper right arm to trap the outside of his arm and seize his wrist with your left hand. Use both hands to Twist [搓, Cuo] it.

2) The left hand can Pull and the right hand can Roll-Back.

3) With your left hand, Pull the opponent's left hand, and the right palm can flash [閃, shan] to his face.

4) The right hand and forearm can first move towards the left and then down and back to Roll-Back, and then bring the right forearm to Press forward. At the same time, the right foot can kick his shinbone.

5) After seizing him, move upward and Break [撅, Jue].

6) Following the joining together, Push and/or kick the opponent's lower extremities.

10) White Crane Cooling Its Wings

白鶴涼翅

Bai He Liang Chi

翅 涼 鶴 白 （10）

From the previous *Lifting-Hands Posture,* raise the right foot with the body following the waist as it turns left. Then place the foot on the ground, slightly flexing the right leg, and plant it firmly (at this point, the body and waist have already turned towards the front left side, internally including the intent of a right Shoulder-Stroke. The right hand is sunk down and to the left, turning it until it arrives below the left elbow, and the left hand is brought to be directly on top of the right elbow. Both hands are simultaneously opened and separated above and below. Take a half-step out with the left foot and bring the toes down to the ground in an Empty Stance. Bring up the right hand to be even with the chest. Fan it open to the right and raise it to the right side of the forehead, with the palm facing outward. At the same time, lower the left hand, Pulling towards the left until reaching the left side of the pelvic area, and turn the palm downward. The distance between the two hands should not be too great.

If there is too much Opening [開, Kai], the intrinsic energy is too easily severed. The body is to follow the movement of the two hands while squatting down. Shift [the weight] into the right leg.

Retain a light and sensitive energy on top of the head. Hollow the chest and raise the back. Draw in the Tail Gateway. Sink the Qi into the lower Elixir Field. The spirit of the eyes gazes to the front. (See Illustration #10.) After the hands Open, they will internally include a Closing Intrinsic Energy [合勁, He Jin].

Illustration #10 Text
Do not be too open, if too open the intrinsic energy will
    be severed.

Applications
1) From the previous *Lifting-Hands Posture* application method, if an opponent uses the left hand to strike your chest, deflect it by raising a hand. If he comes for the head, use the intrinsic energy of Rolling-Back with both hands. But supposing he pulls his left hand away and then from the outside circles in to strike at your right temple [太陽穴,

Tai Yang Xue]. You can use *White Crane Cooling Its Wings* to break it off and attack.

2) If the opponent attacks your right temple with his left hand, use your right arm to hold up and obstruct it. If he follows up with an attack to your stomach with the right fist, move your left hand downwards and to the left, Pulling and Opening. At the same time, use your left foot to kick him in the groin [陰 襠, yin dang].

3) Afterwards, using your left and right hands to obstruct the attacks from both of the opponent's hands, you can then use the intrinsic energy of the waist and legs to issue Ward-Off from your spine, arms, or hands (or initially to Open or after, Close).

11) Brush the Knee and Twist Step (Left Style)
摟膝拗步（左式）
Lou Xi Ao Bu (Zuo Shi)

（式左）步拗膝摟（11）

From the method of *White Crane Cooling Its Wings*, bring the body down into a squat, lodging the center of balance into the right leg. When shifting [sinking] into the right leg, the right hand simultaneously follows the momentum of the waist and legs, first moving downward to the left and then circling back to the right and ascending to the side of the right ear. The left palm, simultaneously, turns until it arrives in front of the chest.

48

The left foot is raised and takes a half-step forward. Bend the left knee. Follow the momentum with the right leg, gradually extending it.

With the left palm (turned downward), move it downward and to the left to brush the knee. At the same time, bring the right hand from beside the right ear and follow the waist and legs to gradually Push out. Seat the waist and squat down, lodging the center of balance in the left leg.

Sink the shoulders and suspend the elbows. Hollow the chest and raise the back. Seat the wrists and extend the fingers. Relax the waist and relax the coccyx. Draw in the Tail Gateway. The eyes gaze and follow the right hand to the front. The body should be upright and centered. Do not lean forward. Suspend the right arm and elbow downward to make them vertical, but not too straight. (See Illustration #11.)

Illustration #11 Text
The [right] arm is not to be too straight.
The body is straight, centered, and upright, without bending
    forward.

Applications
1) From the previous method of *White Crane Cooling Its Wings*, if an opponent attacks your temple with his left hand, use your right arm to hold up and obstruct it, and use your right hand to attack his temple. But supposing he holds up and obstructs with his left hand, you can use your left hand to attack his chest cavity. Supposing the opponent uses his right hand to sweep downward, you then reach downward with your right hand to brush his right arm, and hook his right

foot with your left foot. Simultaneously, return to using your left hand to avail yourself of the momentum towards the right. Then, move directly downwards and to the left to brush the opponent's arm open, pulling out with your right hand and changing it to Push to his chest.

2) If an opponent attacks you with a hand or foot in your middle or lower regions, brush downwards with your left hand and use your right palm to Push their chest cavity.

12) Hands Strum the Lute
手揮琵琶
Shou Hui Pi Pa

琶　琵　揮　手　（12）

From the previous method of *Brush the Knee and Twist Step*
(Left Style), the right-hand palm is to follow the momentum of
the body in bending and crouching down, moving downward
to Push and pat [拍, pai, palming or slapping action].

Raise the right foot and take a half-step forward, shifting
the center of balance onto the right leg.

When raising the upper body, bring the left hand directly
underneath the right elbow before raising both hands to be on
line with the shoulders, separating them to be level with each

other. (Both hands and arms open to complete flat circular shapes.)

Take a half-step forward with the left foot and raise the toes, forming a T-shaped Insubstantial Stance [also known as Seven-Star Stance], then crouch the body down. At the same time, the hands come together as if embracing something, with the right palm directly opposite the left elbow. The left fingers are brought up to the level of the nose. The palms are held uneven and opposite of each other as though appearing to be holding a lute (left hand in front, right hand in back). Bend [the right] knee, seat it so it it substantial while moving the body down into a slight squat. (See Illustration #12.)

Retain a light and sensitive energy on top of the head. Sink the shoulders and suspend the elbows. Hollow the chest and raise the back. Sink the Qi into the lower Elixir Field. Keep the Tail Gateway centered and upright. The spirit of the eyes gazes to the front. The body is not to be too low. The arms are to be relaxed and open. Keep to the mind-intent of Ward-Off so as not to allow the intrinsic energy to be severed.

Illustration #12 Text
The body is not to be too low. If too low the intrinsic energy will be severed.

Applications
1) From the previous application method of *Brush the Knee and Twist Step*, strike the opponent's chest cavity with your right hand. But supposing he brings across his right hand to brush away your hand, then use both hands to avail yourself of the momentum to wrap them around his hand and move it

left. Then take his wrist with your right hand and seize his elbow with your left hand. Use your left foot to hook his foot (or kick his lower region). Use the energy of your waist and legs to make a corresponding twisting movement forward and complete the *Hands Strum the Lute* posture. If he takes a step back, grab his right hand with your left from below, strike his chest again with your right palm, and return to the *Brush the Knee and Twist Step* stance. What if the opponent steps back? Brush his right hand downwards with your left hand. Then bring your right palm to Push and strike his chest cavity, and so again completing the actions of *Brush the Knee and Twist Step*.

2) When an opponent strikes at your chest with his right hand, begin by hollowing your chest to Neutralize [化, Hua], which will slow down his movement. Then wrap around and Adhere [沾, Zhan] to his right wrist with your right hand while also Adhering to his right elbow with your left hand. From this the momentum of your two hands brings the opponent into a conical position by facing him straight on and with mutually turning your hands over into *Hands Strum the Lute* [or simply, *Lifting Hands*]. This may also be done in a left stance.

13) Brush the Knee and Twist Step (One)

捜膝拗步 (一) [Left Style]

Lou Xi Ao Bu (Yi)

（式左）步拗膝捜（ 11 ）

From the posture of *Hands Strum the Lute*, the left palm is turned downwards without moving the left arm. The right hand (palm facing upwards) is extended out to the front until it is below [the level] of the left palm, and so both are opposite of each other.

The two hands rotate, completing a three-dimensional circle [like circling a ball, not a one-dimensional circle]. Both hands are then lowered together (with the right palm dropping and the left hand above). The upper body is then turned towards the right, while simultaneously the hands exchange top and bottom positions. The right hand turns to the back to form half of a three-dimensional circle, raising it to the level of the right ear, palm forward and fingertips pointing upwards. The left hand follows the right hand turning in a circle to the right until it is in front of the right side of the chest.

Raise the left foot and take a half step forward; bend the left knee and follow the momentum by gradually straightening the right leg. Lower the left palm (palm facing downwards) to brush the left knee while the right palm follows from the right ear. Then gradually Push out [with the right arm and hand] to the front with the waist and legs. Seat the waist into a low crouch and so the center of balance is on the left leg.

Illustration #11 Text
The [right] arm is not to be too straight.
The body must be upright and centered, without leaning
    to the front.

Applications
See Posture #11: *Brush the Knee and Twist Step (Left Style).*

14) Brush the Knee and Twist Step (Two)

摟膝拗步 (二) [Right Style]

Lou Xi Ao Bu (Er)

（式右）步拗膝摟（13）

From the previous posture, the center of balance is shifted
to the rear [right leg] and then the tip of the left foot is turned
horizontally to the left. The waist and legs move down towards
left and are then relaxed. The left hand follows the waist, and
then relaxes, circling around to the back and then up to the
left ear level (with the palm facing forward), fingers pointing
upwards. The right hand follows the momentum of turning left
until it is in front of the left side of the chest. Raise the right
foot and take a step forward; bend the right knee and follow

the momentum by gradually straightening the left leg. Lower the right palm (with the palm facing downwards) to brush the right knee while the left palm is brought to the side of the left ear. Gradually towards the front Push out while squatting the waist down and the center of balance is placed on the right leg. (See Illustration #13.)

Continue with the inner workings as described in *Brush the Knee and Twist Step (Left Style)* [Posture #11].

Illustration #13 Text

The [left] arm is not to be too straight.

The body must be upright and centered, without leaning to the front.

Applications

See Posture #11: *Brush the Knee and Twist Step (Left Style)*.

The left and right movements can be interchanged.

15) Brush the Knee and Twist Step (Three)
摟膝拗步 (三) [Left Style]
Lou Xi Ao Bu (San)

(式左) 步拗膝摟 (11)

From the previous posture, the center of balance is shifted to the rear [left] leg and then the tip of the right foot is pivoted horizontally to the right. The waist and legs move down towards the right and then relax. The right hand follows the waist and then relaxes, circling around to the back and then up to the right ear level (with the palm facing forward), fingers pointing upwards. The left hand follows the momentum of turning right until it is in front of the right side of the chest. Raise the left foot and take a step forward; bend the left knee and follow the momentum by gradually straightening the right leg. Lower the left palm (with the palm facing downwards) to brush the left knee while the right palm is brought to the side of the right ear. Gradually towards the front Push out while squatting the waist down and the center of balance is placed on the left leg. (See Illustration #11.)

Continue with the inner workings as described in *Brush the Knee and Twist Step (Left Style)* [Posture #11].

Illustration #11 Text

The [right] arm is not to be too straight.
The body must be upright and centered, without leaning
to the front.

Applications

See Posture #11: *Brush the Knee and Twist Step (Left Style)*.

16) Hands Strum the Lute
手揮琵琶
Shou Hui Pi Pa

琵 琶 揮 手 (12)

See Posture #12.

17) Brush the Knee and Twist Step (Left Style)

摟膝拗步（左式）

Lou Xi Ao Bu (Zuo Shi)

（式左）步拗膝摟（11）

See Posture #11.

18) Swipe Across the Body and Chop

撇身捶

Pie Shen Chui

捶身撇 (14)

From the previous posture, draw the upper body back
slightly and shift the center of balance into the right foot
while changing [turning] the toes of the left foot to the left.
Move the right hand downward to the left, make a fist when
turning and bringing it to head level. Shift the center of
balance to the left foot without moving the right foot, and
bring the right fist down in a chopping motion forward to
the right side (forming a three-dimensional circle), while

simultaneously raising the left hand backwards until its height is level with the waist. (See Illustration #14.)

Relax the waist and coccyx, and the spirit of the eyes gazes forward.

Illustration #14 Text

The grasped fist should be relaxed.

Retain a light and sensitive energy on top of the head.

The body should not lean forward.

Relax the waist and relax the coccyx.

Applications

If an opponent comes in to attack you from the right side, turn your body and initially make a level strike with the right elbow [implying an Elbow-Stroke], then use the right fist to circle around and strike with a chop [捶, chui].

19) Step Forward, Remove, Parry, and Punch
進步搬攔捶
Jin Bu Ban Lan Chui

From *Swipe Across the Body and Chop*, raise the right foot and take a transverse step forwards. Bring the right hand back next to the right side of the waist, and raise the left hand to the level of the left ear. Bring it down and forward, while lowering the upper body and applying downward pressure, until it is flat and horizontal in front of the right side of the chest. Follow with the left foot, shifting it to the left and lifting the heel [making a Coil Stance]. (This is called Remove [搬, Ban]; see Illustration #15.)

Illustration #15 Text
Both arms are to be sunk.
Retain a light and sensitive
    energy on top of the head.
Do not lean the body
    forward.
The Tail Gateway is to be
    centered and upright.

搬 (15)

Stand up and take a step forward with the left foot, slightly bending the left leg and straightening the right while parrying forward with the left palm. (This is called Parry [攔, Lan]; see Illustration #16.)

Illustration #16 Text

攔　(16)

The [right] shoulder should not be held too straight and the elbow should be bent.

Retain a light and sensitive energy on top of the head.

The [right] fist should be relaxed.

The body should be upright and centered.

The right fist follows the upper body downward into a crouch, then strike upwards in a forward circling motion. Do not straighten the right arm too much. At the same time, the left fist circles around, creating half a three-dimensional circle. Bring it back within the right elbow, and do not hold tension in the neck. Keep the gaze forward. (This is called Punch [捶, Chui]; see Illustration #17.)

Illustration #17 Text

[The right arm] is arched and
soft, without extending too
far outward.

捶 (17)

Applications

Your right foot stomps on the opponent's leg while your left
elbow strikes [Elbow-Stroke] his arm; when he attacks with
his right fist, you use your left hand to bring it down [搬, Ban,
Remove]. If his hand rotates out of your own, feint to his chest
by raising your left hand to Parry [攔, Lan] to the left, stepping
up to the left and then strike [捶, Chui, Punch] to his chest with
your right fist.

20) Sealing to Appear As Closing

如封似閉

Ru Feng Si Bi

勿太出 太出勁過

閉 似 封 如 (18)

Proceeding from *Step Forward, Deflect, Parry, and Punch*,
draw back a little and slightly bend the right leg while bringing
[circling] the right fist inwards to the left, then drawing it out,
gradually opening to a palm (facing downwards). At the same
time, the left foot may also follow with a half step. The left
palm faces upward, below the elbow and brachial area of
the right arm, and makes a break to the left (the two hands
intersecting and forming a crooked cross-shape). Then
separate the hands to the left and right, roughly level with

the shoulders (palms outward). Press the waist forwards, but not too far as that will overexert yourself. (If the right foot has already followed, take half a step forward with the left.) Bend the left leg and straighten the right, shifting the weight to the left. (See Illustration #18.)

Keep the neck loose, the body straight, and draw in the Tail Gateway. Sink the Qi into the lower Elixir Field. Hollow the chest and raise the back. Sink the shoulders and suspend the elbows. Seat the wrists and straighten the fingers. Keep the gaze forwards.

Illustration #18 Text
Do not extend too far out, otherwise the intrinsic energy
    will be excessive.

Applications
Proceeding from the use of the previous stance, if somebody grabs your right fist, bring your left hand under the right brachial area and strike their wrist. Draw back your right fist and make a Pushing strike using both palms. This type of Push method is divided into Inner and Outer types.

If an opponent is holding your right fist with his right hand, you can Push his chest cavity (Inner Gate); if he is holding your right fist with his left hand, you can Push it over to the outside of his shoulder [Outer Gate].

21) Embrace Tiger, Return to the Mountain

抱虎歸山

Bao Hu Gui Shan

Proceeding from the previous *Sealing to Appear As Closing* posture, turn the body to the right, the left toes turning inward to the right until they are almost flush with the right foot. Lift the hands upward and spread them to the left and right, then sink into a downward arc by squatting the hips. Bring the hands upward again to join together and make a cross-shape, palms facing inward (as though grasping and lifting an object).

The hands Ward-Off upwards until they are level with the chest and raise the right foot to make a half step to the left. (See Illustration #19.)

Illustration #19 Text

The hands are on line with
　the chest, not too high
　and not too low.

手與胸齊

勿高勿低

（一）山歸虎抱（19）

Turn to the right while the right foot makes a half step to the
right. The hands follow the turning movement and spread
forward and backward, palms facing downward. The right
hand follows the turning of the waist and the squatting of the
body by brushing away to the right. It does not go too low.
Bend the right knee and squat down, shifting the weight to the
right leg and straightening the left leg. (See Illustration #20.)

Illustration #20 Text

The body should not bend
 too far to the front.
Retain a light and sensitive
 energy on top of the head.
Both arms should be sunk.
The [right] hand should not
 be brought too low.

（二）山 歸 虎 抱 (20)

Turn the hips to the right, while striking out with the left hand
across to the right side. (See Illustration #21.)

Illustration #21 Text

Do not lean too much,
as leaning will result in
[extraneous] movement
of the spine.

（三）山 歸 虎 抱（21）

Applications

Proceeding from *Sealing to Appear As Closing*, if the opponent
on the right side strikes downward from above, send your right
arm upward to spread it aside. If he takes advantage of the
gap to attack your chest, cross your hands to Ward-Off his
arm upward (sealing yourself off). If another opponent attacks
with his right fist from your right rear, turn your waist to the
right, stepping out your right foot, and using your right hand
to brush aside his arm (or seize his hand), then attack his
face with your left palm.

If the opponent were to then send his right arm upward to
block your left palm outward, or turns to the left to come back
with an attack to your head, grab his right hand with your left
hand, and perform a Ward-Off strike with your right forearm
or attack his face with your right palm. If he then happens
to neutralize and use his left hand to strike, you could use
Roll-Back, Press, and Push.

71

22) Ward-Off, Roll-Back, Press, and Push

掤 攦 擠 按

Peng Lu Ji An

See Postures #4–7.

23) Diagonal Single Whip
斜單鞭

Xie Dan Bian

See Posture #8, but angled toward the corner.

24) Punch Under Elbow

肘底捶

Zhou Di Chui

捶 底 肘 (22)

From *Diagonal Single Whip*, the hands follow the hips as they turn to the left. The right palm (facing downward) circles around until it is in front of the chest and sinking downward, while the left palm circles to the rear until it's beside the left ribs then threads forward over the right hand to reach upward (the palm edge facing outward, fingers upward).

At the same time, turn and shift the left toes to the left and the right palm grasps into a fist, Tiger's Mouth [虎 口, Hu Kou, crux of the thumb and index finger] facing upward,

which is placed under the left elbow as the right foot
comes forward diagonally a half step and the leg becomes
substantial, and the left foot lifts to be touching down
with the heel, toes lifted, making a T-shaped Empty Stance.
The left elbow must be aligned directly with the left knee so
they are [perpendicular and] not lining up with each other
along a diagonal.

Sink the shoulders and drop the elbows. Keep the head
up without tension and straighten the body. Draw in the
Tail Gateway. (See Illustration #22.)

Illustration #22 Text
The [left] elbow should be on line with the knee.
Do not lean forward nor to the diagonal.

Applications
1) If the opponent attacks with his right hand, bring your
left wrist across to meet his right wrist and Push it aside to
the right, your left fingers hanging down to hook over his wrist.
If he tries to escape by bringing in his left hand, your right
hand goes to the left and sinks down on it. With both his
hands sealed off, use your left palm to attack his face or do
a finger jab to his throat, and your right fist striking forward
to his chest.

2) If the opponent attacks with his right hand, grab his
right elbow with your left hand, draw him in, then turn your
wrist over, propping upward and away, and use your right
fist to attack his chest or ribs.

3) If the opponent's left hand comes across to attack your
right temple, seize it with your left hand and return a strike

with your right hand to his left temple. If he tries to lift his left arm up, press it down with your right forearm and make your left hand into a fist to attack his chin.

25) Moving Backwards to Chase the Monkey Away (Right Style)

倒攆猴 (右 式)

Dao Nian Hou (You Shi)

(式右) 猴攆倒 (23)

From *Punch Under Elbow*, turn the waist and legs to the right as the right fist becomes a palm and follows the hips by circling downward and to the rear (the gaze following the hand) then turns over and goes upward until beside the right ear.

At the same time, the left palm comes forward with a sinking Push, while the left foot retreats a step, and the knee bends. The leg becomes substantial as the right leg becomes insubstantial. The right palm follows the movement by pushing forward as the left palm correspondingly turns over and draws back to the rear to be placed beside the left hip. The weight is on the left leg.

Keep the head up without tension and straighten the body. Sink the shoulders and drop the elbows. Seat the wrists and straighten the fingers. Sink the Qi into the lower Elixir Field. Keep the spirit of the gaze forward. (See Illustration #23.)

Illustration #23 Text
The body must be upright without too much leaning
    to the front.

Applications
1) Proceeding from the use of *Punch Under Elbow,* if the opponent pushes up your right fist with his left hand and grabs your left hand with his right hand, first send your left palm forward with a sinking Push, drawing it back as your left leg retreats, while your right fist becomes a palm and follows the turning of your hips by first Neutralizing [化, Hua] to the rear, then circling upward beside your right ear, and Pushing out forward.

2) If the opponent strikes with his right hand, advancing fiercely, Withdraw Step your left leg while blocking downward with your left hand and striking his face with your right palm.

26) Moving Backwards to Chase the Monkey Away (Left Style)

倒 攆 猴 (左 式)

Tao Nian Hou (Zuo Shi)

（ 式左 ）猴攆倒 (24)

From the previous posture, the torso turns to the left as the left palm circles downward and to the rear (the gaze following the hand) then turns over and goes upward until beside the left ear. At the same time, the right palm comes forward with a sinking Push, while the right foot retreats a step, and the knee bends, the leg becoming substantial as the left leg becomes empty. The left palm follows the movement by Pushing forward, the right palm turning over and correspondingly drawing back to the rear to be placed beside the right hip. The rest is the same as in the previous posture [but with the weight on the right leg].

When practicing *Moving Backwards to Chase the Monkey Away*, you may retreat three, five, or seven steps. All that matters is that the last one ends on the right side. (See Illustration #24.)

Illustration #24 Text
The eyes gaze at the hand.
Sink the Qi into the lower Elixir Field.

Applications
Same as with the right style, only with the left and right hands and legs reversed.

Chen Kung's Note
In the old frame of the Tai Ji Quan set, the hands in *Moving Backwards to Chase the Monkey Away* withdraw only to be beside the hips and do not circle any farther to the rear.

27) Diagonal Flying Posture

斜飛勢

Xie Fei Shi

身勿前俯

膝勿出足头

勢 飛 斜 (25)

From the previous posture, *Moving Backwards to Chase the Monkey Away,* the left palm follows the hips by going forward and downward, shifting the weight gradually to the right leg, and reaches forward (the palm facing upward) below the right palm (facing downward). The hands turn over together, the left palm circling around until it is above the right palm, as the left foot takes a sideways step to the left, and with the hands seeming to be holding a ball, they follow the hips by extending out to the left in unison, left hand above, right hand below, shifting the weight to the left leg. The hands then follow the hips by turning to the right until in front of the chest, left palm facing downward, right hand circling around until it is under the left elbow (palm facing upward), the palms facing each other, as the left toes turn inward to the right. The right foot steps out to the right, and the knee gradually bends, the leg becoming substantial as the left leg straightens, the hands spreading apart in unison to the front and rear, right hand Warding-Off forward and upward (palm facing upward), left hand seizing downward to the rear (palm facing downward).

Keep the spirit of the eyes on the right hand. Shift the weight to the right leg, but the knee should not pass over the toes. The body should not lean forward. Sink the shoulders and suspend the elbows. (See Illustration #25.)

Illustration #25 Text
The body is not to lean to the front.
Do not let the [right] knee pass over the toes.

Applications
Proceeding from the use of *Moving Backwards to Chase the Monkey Away (Right Style)*, if the opponent spreads aside your right palm with his left hand, jab to his solar plexus with your left fingers. If he props this up from below with his left hand, Neutralize [化 勁, Hua Jin] by scooping underneath with your right hand, then attack his chest with both palms in unison. If he then attacks with his left hand, turn your waist to the right, seizing and plucking his hand with your left hand, and step forward with your right foot. Your right arm performs Ward-Off by going forward, upward, and across.

28) Lifting Hands Posture

提手上勢

Ti Shou Shang Shi

（9）提手上勢

See Posture #9.

29) White Crane Cooling Its Wings
白鶴涼翅

Bai He Liang Chi

翅涼鶴白（10）

See Posture #10.

30) Brush the Knee and Twist Step (Left Style)
摟膝拗步（左式）
Lou Xi Ao Bu (Zuo Shi)

（式左）步拗膝摟（11）

See Posture #11.

31) Needle at Sea Bottom
海底針
Hai Di Zhen

針 底 海 (26)

From *Brush the Knee and Twist Step (Left Style),* the right palm follows the drawing back of the hips by first going downward, to the rear, and then circling upward until in front of the chest, the right foot coming forward a half step, the right palm facing to the left, the edge of the palm hooking to the rear, fingers hanging down, and the left hand near the right elbow.

As the right knee bends and the leg becomes substantial, the left foot Withdraw Steps a half step, toes touching down, making an Empty Stance, and the hands sink down as you bend at the waist. The breath sinks into the lower abdomen. Keep the gaze forward. (See Illustration #26.)

Illustration #26 Text
The [left] knee is not to go too far outwards.

Applications
1) Proceeding from the use of *Brush the Knee and Twist Step (Left Style)*, if the opponent sinks your right palm down with his left hand and strikes your head with his right hand, first ward away his right arm with your left forearm while your right hand circles around from below to the outside of your left forearm and goes upward to seize his right wrist (or elbow), then use power from your hips to pluck down. If he were to resist upward, you could follow his momentum by performing *Fan Penetrates the Back,* your right hand lifting and the left palm striking pressure points on his torso.

2) If the opponent grabs your right wrist with his right hand, your left hand covers the back of his hand, the edge of your right palm goes upward to the left and circles around to hook his right wrist, then your hands follow your waist and legs by seizing downward, causing his feet to leave the ground as he topples forward, the seize also jolting his head, producing dizziness.

32) Fan Penetrates the Back

扇通背

Shan Tong Bei

背 通 扇 （27）

From *Needle at Sea Bottom*, the hands follow the hips by rising up, the right palm Warding-Off upward and outward, the palm turning over to face outward, the palm edge facing upward, until beside the right temple, the left palm rising until in front of the chest, the palm facing outward.

Push out forward as the left foot steps forward, toes pointing forward, and the leg becomes substantial as the hips advance, the right leg gradually straightening.

Sink the shoulders and suspend the elbows. Seat the wrists and straighten the fingers. Relax the waist and coccyx. Draw in the Tail Gateway. Keep the body upright. The intrinsic energy is issued from the spine. The spirit of the eyes gazes forward. (See Illustration #27.)

Illustration #27 Text

The body is to be centered and upright, without leaning to
the front, and the intrinsic energy is issued from the spine.

Applications

1) Proceeding from the use of *Needle at Sea Bottom,* in which your right hand seized the opponent's right hand, sinking downward with power from your waist, if he lifts his right arm upward, take advantage of the momentum by Warding-Off his hand upward and outward with your right hand, then as your left foot steps forward and your hips advance, your left palm strikes his waist.

2) If the opponent strikes with his right hand, turn over your right hand, drawing his right wrist upward, and Ward-Off outward while striking the right side of his waist with your left palm.

33) Turn Body, Swipe Across Body and Chop
轉身撇身捶
Zhuan Shen Pie Shen Chui

From the previous posture, *Fan Penetrates the Back,* the hands go upward as the hips turn to the right, the left toes turning to the right, and once the hands are to the right, the right hand gradually grasps into a fist (Tiger's Mouth facing upward) and does a level strike across to the left, the left palm Warding-Off upward to be placed in front of the forehead. The hands then follow the rightward turning of the hips, the right fist (the back of the fist facing upward) is sideways in front of the chest with the left palm still in front of the forehead. (See Illustration #28.)

Illustration #28 Text
The [right] fist should not extend out too far, and [the body] must be centered and upright.

（一）捶身撇身轉（28）

The right foot steps diagonally forward to the right as the right fist turns over (center of the fist facing upward), flinging upward, forward, and down, while the left hand is placed over the inside of the right elbow. The right fist withdraws to be beside the right side of the waist as the left hand strikes out forward. (See Illustration #29.)

Illustration #29 Text
The body is not to lean
    too much.
Seek to follow the
    momentum.

（二）捶身撇身轉（29）

Applications
If the opponent attacks from the right side, turn the body to the right and use the right elbow to strike across at him. Then, use the right fist to drag down his hand. Take advantage of the opportunity to strike his face with the left palm.

34) Step Forward, Remove, Parry, and Punch
進步搬攔捶
Jin Bu Ban Lan Chui

捶 攔 搬 步 進 (30)

From the previous posture of *Turn Body, Swipe Across Body and Chop*, the right fist (Tiger's Mouth facing upward) follows the hips by striking out to the right as the left palm withdraws to the inside of the right elbow. Then both hands follow the hips by Rolling-Back downward to the left rear, the right foot lifting and stepping down inward and turned out sideways. The body squats down with the left knee bending over the right lower leg, the hips turning to the right, as you bend the left elbow to put the arm across in front of the chest (palm facing downward), the right elbow bending to put the hand below the left hand (palm facing upward) [see Illustration #15. Note that in this posture the movements of illustrations #15 and #16 occur in the same direction as Illustration #30].

Then the left palm strikes forward [see Illustration #16], withdraws to the inside of the right elbow as the left foot steps forward and the right fist strikes out (Tiger's Mouth facing upward) [see Illustration #30]. The rest is the same as in Posture #19. (See Illustration #30.)

搬 (15) 攔 (16)

Illustration #30 Text

The body is not to lean forward.

Suspend the [right] elbow.

The [right] arm is slightly bent and not to be straightened.

The [right] fist is upright and on line [with the shoulder] and
is slightly relaxed.

35) Step Forward to Ward-Off, Roll-Back, Press, and Push

上步掤擺擠按

Shang Bu Peng Lu Ji An

掤（4）　　　　擺（5）

擠（6）　　　　按（7）

Proceeding from *Step Forward, Remove, Parry, and Punch,* the hands follow the waist and legs by moving inward to the [right] then downward to the [left] to make a complete circle as the right foot steps forward, then use the intrinsic energy from the waist and legs to Ward-Off forward and upward. The rest is the same as in the four postures of #4–7.

36) Single Whip

單鞭

Dan Bian

鞭單 (8)

See Posture #8.

37) Cloud Hands
雲手
Yun Shou

From the posture of *Single Whip,* the left palm follows the
waist and legs by circling to the right until in front of the chest,
then to the left and downward until in front of the abdomen
(palm facing up). At the same time, the right-hand palm
(facing down) circles downward to the left, then rises from
the left side of the abdomen, Warding-Off upward to the right
until below the right side of the jaw (palm facing inward). The
left toes follow the movement by turning inward to the right to
be almost parallel with the right foot and the right foot takes a
half step sideways to the left (the weight is now in both feet).
(See Illustration #31.)

Illustration #31 Text
The body should not
   be seated too low.
The upper body must
   be centered and
   upright.
Both hands are fashioned
   like holding a sphere.

（一）手 雲 (31)

The right foot takes a half step sideways to the left to stand next to the left foot. With both knees bent and the body squatting. The right hand follows the hips by continuing to the right and Pushing down, fulfilling a complete circle, as the left hand goes to the right and upward, Warding-Off until level with the right side of the chest. (See Illustration #32.)

Illustration #32 Text

Retain a light and sensitive
    energy on top of the head.
The entire body should be
    centered and upright.
Draw in the Tail Gateway.
The spirit of the eyes gazes
    to the front.
The [right] hand has a Pushing
    and sinking downward
    momentum.

（二）手 雲 （32）

As the left hand rises past the lower jaw, the right hand circles until in front of the chest and the left foot takes a half step sideways to the left that is first empty, then becomes substantial. (See Illustration #33.)

Illustration #33 Text

Both hands should not be held too high.

The body should not be seated too low.

The upper body must be centered and upright.

(三) 手 雲 (33)

The left hand follows the hips by continuing to the left and Pushing down, fulfilling a complete circle, as the right hand circles upward from below and the right foot takes a half step sideways to the left. The hands follow the hips, moving up and down, left and right, rising and falling, Warding-Off and Pushing, like two wheels turning, as the feet constantly step sideways to the left, the movements repeating over and over.

The body should not squat too low. The upper body should be upright. The Tail Gateway should be tucked in. The gaze follows the circling of the right hand as it Wards-Off and Pushes, then with the left hand as it Wards-Off and Pushes. Clouding with the hands to the left and right can be performed three, five, or seven times.

When it changes to another *Single Whip* posture, the left hand first circles to the right, along with the hips, to be level with the right hand. The hands (palms facing downward) then arc to the left and sink downward until in front of the chest, then the fingers of both hands poke out to the right as the left foot steps diagonally to the left corner, and the left palm passes the face and Pushes out, the right hand now shaped as a hook, making the Single Whip.

Applications
When the opponent's hand attacks, your hand Wards-Off to Neutralize [化, Hua] and Push it away, or you use one hand to Neutralize with a Ward-Off and the other hand to attack with a palm strike.

In this practice during Warding-Off, it is said that inside the body there is the "mixing of the Qi from the liver and lungs."

38) Single Whip

單鞭

Dan Bian

See Posture #8.

39) High Pat on Horse

高探馬

Gao Cai Ma

手掌勿太高過首

馬 探 高 (34)

From the previous posture of *Single Whip*, the right foot follows the waist and legs to advance by lifting [the leg] and then stepping down a half step forward, while the left hand relaxes and sinks.

The right palm (facing down) circles to the left, upward, and forward. At the same time, the left foot slightly moves back, toes touching down, and the left palm (facing upward) draws back until in front of the chest, the right knee slightly bending, and the weight settling in the right leg.

Hollow the chest and raise the back. Relax the waist and coccyx. Keep the spirit of the gaze forward. Retain a light and sensitive energy on top of the head. The body should not lean forward. The right palm extends forward in connection with the lower back. (See Illustration #34.)

Illustration #34 Text
The palm of the hand should not be held too high and not
    pass above the head.

Applications
1) Your left hand seizes the opponent's left hand (or the back of your left wrist flops onto his hand) while your right palm strikes his face.

2) Your right hand follows the rightward turning of your hips by grabbing the opponent's right fist and your left hand jabs to the right side of his waist (as you sit down onto your left leg). If he adjusts to this, instead seize downward with your right hand, your left hand circling upward to jab to his throat. If his left hand then comes out to intercept, step forward with your right foot as your left hand grabs his left wrist, and use your right forearm to break his arm.

40) Separate Foot, Right
右分脚

You Fen Jiao

From *High Pat on Horse,* the hands follow the waist and legs by circling forward to the right, then Rolling-Back to the left rear until in front of the left side of the chest. The left foot takes a half step out to the forward left corner and the weight shifts to the left leg, the hands again circling to the right and Rolling-Back to the left rear. (See Illustration #35.)

Illustration #35 Text
The toes point to the front.
The body should not be
　moved too far back.

:（一）脚 分 右（35）

The right foot takes a half step to the forward left corner, toes touching down, heel lifted, as the hands arc upward in front of the chest, embracing inward to make an X shape. The palms then turn over to face downward and spread apart to the sides at shoulder level as the body rises and the right foot toe kicks to the right corner, the left leg slightly bent and with all the weight on it.

Retain a light and sensitive energy on top of the head. Hollow the chest and raise the back. The right toes are pointed forward. The body should not lean too far back. Keep the spirit of the gaze to the right front side. (See Illustration #36.)

Illustration #36 Text

The toes of the foot faces the front.
The body should not move too far back.

（二）踢 分 右（36）

Applications

1) From the use of *High Pat on Horse*, if the opponent's left hand connects to your right palm, grab his left wrist with your left hand, then place your right forearm behind his left elbow and Roll-Back to the left. If he Neutralizes [化, Hua] by Pulling Back and then attacks with his right hand, send both your hands up to lift it away, then chop down forward with your right hand while stabbing a right toe kick to his solar plexus or left ribs.

2) If the opponent grabs your left arm and is about to break it, circle your right arm to follow your hips, coming around from below to the outside of his right elbow, then grab his elbow and take advantage of the opportunity to stab a right toe kick to his right ribs.

41) Separate Foot, Left

左分脚

Zuo Fen Jiao

From *Separate Foot, Right,* the right foot comes down to the forward right corner. Bend the knee and shift the weight to the right leg, the hands going along with the hips by Rolling-Back to the right rear.

Hollow the chest and raise the back. Keep the spirit of the gaze forward. (See Illustration #37.)

Illustration #37 Text

The toes of the foot
    face the front.
The position of the hands
    and feet are to be
    on line.

（一）脚分左（37）

The hands Roll-Back until in front of the chest, then follow the hips by circling to the forward left, and again Rolling-Back to the right rear. The left foot takes a half step to the forward right corner, toes touching down, heel lifted, as the hands arc upward in front of the chest, embracing inward to make an

X shape. The palms then turn over to face downward and spread apart to the sides at shoulder level as the body rises and the left foot toe kicks to the left corner, the right leg slightly bent and with all the weight on it.

Keep the head up without tension. Draw back the chest and straighten the back. The body should not lean too far back. Keep the gaze to the left front side. (See Illustration #38.)

Illustration #38 Text
The toes of the foot
    face the front.
The momentum of the
    hands and feet are
    on line.

（二）脚 分 左（38）

Applications

1) If the opponent attacks with his right hand, grab his right wrist with your right hand and Roll-Back his right arm with your left forearm. If he Neutralizes [化, Hua] by Pulling Back and then attacks with his left hand, send both your hands up to lift it away, then chop down and forward with your left hand while stabbing a left toe kick to his solar plexus or right ribs.

2) If the opponent grabs your right arm and is about to break it, your left hand follows your hips, circling to the right and coming around from below to grab to the outside of his left elbow and stab a left toe kick to his left ribs.

42) Turn Body and Kick With the Sole
轉身蹬腳

Zhuan Shen Deng Jiao

脚 蹬 身 轉 (39)

From *Separate Foot, Left,* the left foot withdraws, knee still lifted (toes hanging down), and the hands embrace inward to make an X shape (left hand on the outside, right hand on the inside, palms facing inward).

The right heel slightly lifts and the ball of the foot pivots along with the waist as it turns to the left (making a one quarter turn) while the palms go downward, turning over to face outward. The body should not lean forward.

Once the body has turned and settled, slightly squat and then rise up, doing a level pressing kick forward with the left heel while spreading the hands apart at shoulder level.

Keep the head up without tension. Draw back the chest and straighten the back. Eyes gaze forward. (See Illustration #39.)

Illustration #39 Text
The body is not to be held too high.
The position of the hands and feet are on line.

Applications
1) Proceeding from *Separate Foot, Left,* if the opponent attacks you from behind, turn around to defend, taking advantage of the opportunity to do a pressing kick to his belly with your left foot while striking his face with your left hand (which can also be used to prevent him from brushing aside your left leg).

2) If the opponent strikes your face, go with it by leaning back to Neutralize [化, Hua] while propping away his hand with your left hand and doing a pressing kick to his belly or waist with your left foot.

43) Left and Right Brush Knee and Twist Step
左右摟膝拗步 (左式)
Lou Xi Ao Bu

身宜中正
勿前俯

臂勿太直

步 拗 膝 摟 左 (40)

[Left Style]
From the previous posture, *Turn Body and Kick With Sole,*
the left foot comes down forward and to the left, the left hand
follows the hips by brushing to the left past the left knee, the
left knee bending, the leg becomes substantial, and the right
palm is Pushing out to the front. (See Illustration #40.)

Illustration #40 Text
The body must be upright and centered and not leaning
   to the front.
Sink the shoulders and suspend the elbows.

[Right Style]

The right foot takes a step forward, the right hand follows the hips by brushing to the right past the right knee, the right knee bending, the leg becomes substantial, and the left palm is Pushing out to the front. The rest is the same as in Postures #13 and #14. (See Illustration #41.)

步 拗 膝 摟 右（41）

Illustration #41 Text

The body must be upright and centered, and not leaning
    to the front.
Sink the shoulders and suspend the elbow.

44) Advance Step to Plant Punch
進步栽捶

Jin Bu Zai Chui

捶 栽 步 進（42）

From *Left and Right Brush Knee and Twist Step,* the right toes turn and shift across to the right, the waist and legs moving to the right and relaxing downward to the rear. The right hand moves alongside the hip by circling in a horizontal circle outward and to the right, grasping into a fist (Tiger's Mouth facing upward), and is placed beside the right hip, while the left hand is going along with the waist and legs by circling to the right until in front of the chest. The left foot Advance Steps forward, gradually the knee bends, and the left hand brushes downward past the left knee and is placed beside the left hip. At the same time, the right fist goes forward and downward with a Planting Punch, and the right leg follows the stance by gradually straightening.

Relax the waist and coccyx. Retain a light and sensitive energy on top of the head. Hollow the chest and raise the back. Keep the spirit of the eyes gazing to the front. (See Illustration #42.)

Illustration #42 Text

The body should not lean too far forward.
The [left] knee should not pass over the toes.

Applications

1) Proceeding from the use of *Right Brush Knee and Twist Step*, if the opponent uses his left foot to kick to your belly, first send your right hand upward to block it to the left. He will surely lean to the left, so follow up by stepping forward with your left foot, brushing aside with your left hand, and using your right fist to strike downward.

2) If the opponent uses his right fist to attack your chest, use your right hand to block it to the left, your left hand to brush it aside, and then use your right fist to strike downward.

45) Turn Body, Swipe Across Body and Chop

轉身撇身捶

Zhuan Shen Pie Shen Chui

（一）捶身撇身轉（43）

[First Part, Chop]

From the posture of *Advance Step to Plant Punch*, both hands rise up, following the waist and legs with turning to the right. The left toes are also turned and moved to the right. The remainder is similar to the inner workings of Posture [#34].

The right fist comes to a momentary stop (see Illustration #43), and then moves upwards and to the rear (moving the forearm, but not the upper arm).

Illustration #43 Text

The fist must by grasped in a relax manner.

The arm must be slightly bent.

Retain a light and sensitive energy on top of the head.

Hollow the chest and raise the back.

The body must be upright and centered.

[Second Part, Punch]

Flip the elbow so it is beside [on line with] the right shoulder, and the left palm moves ahead and upwards, then circles back around the right fist and returns to its original position. Meanwhile, the right fist strikes forward beneath the left palm (Tiger's Mouth facing upwards; see Illustration #44) and then opens to a downward facing palm as the left palm flips upwards. Swing the two hands back and to the left. For the remainder, see Posture #34.

Illustration #44 Text

The elbow must be
    slightly bent.

The fist must by grasped
    in a relax manner.

Retain a light and sensitivity
    on top of the head.

The Tail Gateway must be
    centered and upright.

（二）捶身撇身轉（44）

Applications

Your right fist blocks the opponent. If he uses his hands to raise your fist, you utilize his strength to move up and back, returning the fist to its original position. Your left hand moves up, raising his hand and allowing your right fist to strike his chest or flank.

46) Step Forward, Remove, Parry, and Punch
進步搬攔捶

Jin Bu Ban Lan Chui

（二）捶身撇身轉（44）

See Posture #34 [or Posture #19, which shows the illustrations going in this direction].

47) Kick With Right Foot

右踢脚

You Ti Jiao

手足勢平
手勿太高

脚 踢 右 （45）

From *Step Forward, Remove, Parry, and Punch,* the left toes
turn to the left (to be pointing to the left), and the weight
gradually shifts to the left leg, as the palms spread apart to the
sides and go downward (palms facing downward), relaxing
and sinking until in front of the belly with the palms turning
upward as they come together. The hands lift upward while
embracing inward to make an X shape (palms facing inward)
as the right foot goes forward a half step, toes touching down,
heel lifted. The hands in unison turn over to face downward,

then spread apart to the sides at shoulder level, with the upper body relaxing as the right foot toe kicks upward to the right corner.

Retain a light and sensitive energy on top of the head and straighten the body. Draw in the Tail Gateway. Hollow the chest and raise the back. Keep the spirit of the gaze forward to the right front side. (See Illustration #45.)

Illustration #45 Text
The position of the [right] hand and foot must be on line.
The [right] hand is not to be held too high.

Applications
Do a right toe kick upward to the opponent's wrist. The rest is the same as in Posture #40, except this kick is directly ahead.

Chen Kung's Note
In the old frame of the Tai Ji Quan set, *Advance Step to Plant Punch* was followed by [a posture called] *Turn Around and Double Kick,* then *Retreat Step to Strike Tiger Stance (Right Style).* But most people nowadays have given up doing it this way, substituting the double kick with the three postures of *Turn Body, Swipe Across Body and Chop* then *Step Forward, Remove, Parry, and Punch,* then *Kick With Right Foot,* and this is because the double kick was not easy to practice.

48) Strike Tiger, Left
左打虎

Zuo Da Hu

虎 打 左 （46）

From the previous posture, *Kick With Right Foot,* the right foot comes down almost next to the left foot and the left foot steps to the left rear as the hands Roll-Back downward to the left rear then rise up. Making a circle to the right then back to the left, the right palm circles until in front of the chest, grasping into a fist (Tiger's Mouth facing inward, the center of the fist facing downward), the left palm circles upward until beside the left temple, also grasping into a fist (the center of the fist facing outward).

As the torso turns to the left, the right fist circles across to the left to be beside the left ribs, the left leg gradually bending at the knee and becoming substantial, the legs making a diagonal Bow Stance.

Keep the head up without tension. Sink the shoulders and hollow the chest. Relax the waist and hips. The Tail Gateway is centered. Keep the gaze forward. (See Illustration #46.)

Illustration #46 Text
The entire body must be upright and centered.
The knee must not pass over the toes.

Applications
1) If the opponent strikes your chest with his left fist, Neutralize [化, Hua] by dodging your body sideways, bringing your right hand across to grab his wrist (or elbow) and pluck downward to the left, while striking your left fist upward to his right temple.

2) If the opponent props up your left elbow and uses his right shoulder to bump and strike pressure points on your left flank, you can send your right hand upward to grab his right elbow, lifting your left foot and placing it behind him, and strike him from behind with your left fist.

3) If the opponent tries to break your left arm with his right arm, you can also use the above method.

49) Strike Tiger, Right
右 打 虎
You Da Hu

虎 打 右 (47)

From *Strike Tiger, Left,* the right foot lifts and takes a half step to the right rear, the hands going along with the hips as they turn to the right. (As the fists arc, they will first open into palms, then afterwards become fists.) The left hand is going to the left and downward, then making a large arc to the right and upward until in front of the left side of the chest, held into a fist (Tiger's Mouth facing inward, the center of the fist facing downward), while the right hand is circling downward to the right, then rising until beside the right temple, also grasping into a fist (the center of the fist facing outward). As the torso turns to the right, the left fist circles across to the right to be beside the right ribs, the right leg gradually bending at the knee and becoming substantial, the legs making a diagonal Bow Stance. The rest is the same as in the previous posture. (See Illustration #47.)

Illustration #47 Text
The [right] knee must not pass over the toes.
The body is not to lean too much.

Applications
1) Proceeding from the use of the left side, the opponent to your right strikes the right side of your waist with his left fist (or does a right toe kick to your lower body). Block aside to the right and downward with your right hand. If he withdraws his left fist and switches to striking your chest with his right fist, brush it away downward with your left hand while sending your right fist up and around to attack his head.

2) If the opponent props up your right elbow with his left hand and uses his [left] shoulder to bump and strike pressure points on your right flank, you can send your left hand upward to grab his left elbow, drawing back your right foot and placing it behind him, and strike him from behind with your right fist.

3) If the opponent tries to break your right arm with his left arm, you can also use the above method.

Chen Kung's Note

The old frame of the Yang Tai Ji Quan set has only the *Strike Tiger, Right* and did not perform the left posture. Instead continuing directly into *Kick With Right Foot*. After *Strike Tiger, Right* the hands would first make an X shape [crossing hands gesture] rising until in front of the chest, then spreading to the sides and downward (palms facing downward), relaxing and sinking to the level of the lower abdomen. The rest is as in the following *Kick With Right Foot* posture.

50) Kick With Right Foot

右 踢 脚

You Ti Jiao

脚 踢 右 （45）

From the posture of *Strike Tiger, Right*, the hands follow the leftward turning of the hips, the left toes turning to the left (to be pointing to the left), and the weight gradually shifts to the left leg, the knee bending and leg becoming substantial as the right leg gradually straightens, making an Empty Stance. The hands join to make an X shape [crossing hands gesture] rising until in front of the chest. They then spread apart and go downward (palms facing downward), relaxing and sinking until in front of the belly with the palms turning upward as they come together, and lift upward while embracing inward to again make an X shape. The rest is the same as in Posture #47.

Illustration #45 Text

The [right] hand and foot are positioned to be on line. The [right] hand is not to be held too high.

Applications

Proceeding from the use of *Strike Tiger, Right,* if the opponent attacks from the left with his right hand, send your hands to the left and upward with an X shape to brace it away, then feint an attack to his face with your right hand while sending a toe kick upward to his wrist.

51) Double Winds to Both Ears

雙風貫耳

Shuang Feng Guan Er

耳貫風雙 (48)

From *Kick With Right Foot*, after the right toes have kicked forward and upward, the foot promptly withdraws, the knee staying lifted, toes hanging down (not touching down yet), and the body slightly withdraws, sitting on the left leg, while the palms (facing upward) go along the sides of the right knee and withdraw until beside the hips, becoming fists.

The right foot comes down forward and gradually the knee bends, the leg becoming substantial, as the left leg extends, becoming empty, while the fists go forward, upward, and toward each other (Tiger's Mouths facing each other, the centers of the fists facing outward) to be about a foot apart.

Retain a light and sensitive energy on top of the head. Hollow the chest and raise the back. Sink the shoulders and relax the waist. Keep the spirit of the gaze to the front. (See Illustration #48.)

Illustration #48 Text
The fists must not be passed over too high.
The fists keep a distance from each other, not being too near.

Applications
1) If the opponent uses both fists (or palms) to attack your chest (or belly), spread his wrists away to the sides using the backs of your hands, sinking down to the rear, your hands become fists and go upward to attack his ears (or temples) with the Tiger's Mouths.

2) If the opponent pushes on one of your arms with both hands, lean away until you cannot Neutralize [化, Hua] him any further, then send your other hand up from below, threading between his hands, and while your hips are Neutralizing to the rear, spread his hands apart with both of your hands, then attack his temples with fists.

52) Kick With Left Foot

左踢脚

Zuo Ti Jiao

脚 踢 左 (49)

From the previous posture, *Double Winds to Both Ears,* the fists become palms which spread apart at shoulder level then relax and sink downward until in front of the belly (palms facing downward) as the right toes turn out to the right (to point to the right corner).

The palms turn upward, coming together, and go upward, embracing inward to make an X shape (palms facing inward) as the left foot goes forward to the right side to stand a half step in front of the right foot, toes touching down, heel lifted.

The palms in unison turn to face downward and spread apart to the sides at shoulder level, the body rising, as the left foot comes up and does a toe kick to the left corner.

Retain a light and sensitive energy on top of the head. Hollow the chest and raise the back. The Tail Gateway is centered. Keep the spirit of the gaze to the front left side. (See Illustration #49.)

Illustration #49 Text
The hand and foot must be positioned on line.

Applications
Do a toe kick to the opponent's wrist, elbow, or flank with your left foot.

53) Turn Body and Kick With the Sole

轉身蹬腳

Zhuan Shen Deng Jiao

脚 蹬 身 轉 (50)

From *Kick With Left Foot,* the left foot withdraws, knee still lifted (toes hanging down), as the hands embrace inward to make an X shape (left hand on the outside, right hand on the inside).

The right heel is slightly raised and the whole body spins in a large half circle [to the right] on the ball of the foot (making a three-quarter turn).

When the [left] foot comes down, sit fully on it and squat the body as the hands come downward, turning inward. Then when the palms have turned to first face downward then outward, do a level pressing kick forward with the right heel while spreading the hands apart at shoulder level.

Retain a light and sensitive energy on top of the head. Hollow the chest and raise the back. Keep the spirit of the gaze to the front right side. (See Illustration #50.)

Illustration #50 Text
The bottom of the foot presses out levelly.

Applications
Proceeding from the use of *Kick With Left Foot*, once you have kicked with your left foot, if the opponent tries to pull on your foot, immediately withdraw it, and if he chases forward to attack again, spin around to the right to evade it. At the perfect instant, settle onto your left foot, squatting your body with an energy of storing, then take advantage of the opportunity to Stick [黏, Nian] to (or seize) his elbow or wrist with your right hand and do a pressing kick with your right foot to his ribs (or belly). This is quite an ingenious method of seizing victory on the cusp of defeat.

54) Swipe Across the Body and Chop

撇身捶

Pie Shen Chui

捶 身 撇 （14）

From *Turn Body and Kick With the Sole,* the right foot withdraws as the hips turn to the left, and the right palm goes to the right just like Roll-Back, facing downward, then circles to the left, gradually grasping into a fist (the back of the fist facing upward), drawing back to the left until in front of the left side of the chest, then circles upward and forward, the wrist turning over, and flings downward (so the center of the fist is facing upward).

At the same time, the right foot Cross Steps and is placed on the ground (i.e. toes pointing to the right, heel pointing to the left, instep facing to the outside). The left hand circles to the rear then comes forward to be placed above the inside of the right elbow just like Roll-Back. The rest is the same as in Posture #18.

55) Step Forward, Remove, Parry, and Punch

進步搬攔捶

Jin Bu Ban Lan Chui

搬 （15）

攔 （16）   捶 （17）

See Posture #19.

56) Sealing to Appear As Closing

如封似閉

Ru Feng Si Bi

閉似封如 (18)

See Posture #20.

57) Embrace Tiger, Return to the Mountain

抱虎歸山

Bao Hu Gui Shan

（一）山歸虎抱（19）

（二）山歸虎抱（20）

（三）山歸虎抱（21）

See Posture #21.

58) Ward-Off, Roll-Back, Press, and Push
掤擺擠按

Peng Lu Ji An

掤 （4） 擺 （5）

擠 （6） 按 （7）

See Postures #4–7.

59) Horizontal Single Whip

橫單鞭

Heng Dan Bian

鞭 單 橫 (51)

From the previous postures of *Ward-Off, Roll-Back, Press, and Push,* the left foot takes a half step to the front left side and the body is facing directly forward. (See Illustration #51.) The rest is the same as in Posture #8.

Illustration #51 Text

The rear hand is not to be held too high.

The body is to be centered and upright, and not leaning
  to the front.

60) Wild Horse Parting Its Mane (Right Style)

野馬分鬃 (右式)

Ye Ma Fen Zong (You Shi)

高太直太勿手 身勿太偏 膝勿伸出足尖

(式右) 鬃分馬野 (52)

From the previous posture, *Horizontal Single Whip*, the left palm (palm edge downward, then palm facing upward) follows the hips by circling inward to the right, as the right hand (palm edge downward, then palm facing downward) correspondingly circles inward to the left, the left toes turning to the right.

Once the right hand has arced and fully extended to the left (palm facing downward), then circles outward to the right (palm edge downward) as the left hand (palm facing downward) correspondingly circles to the left, and once it has gone its full extent to the left, it then goes outward to the right, facing downward in front of the chest, the right foot stepping out a half step to the right.

The knee gradually bends and the leg becomes substantial, the left leg gradually straightening, as the hands spread apart in unison above and below, the right arm Warding-Off upward diagonally to the right while the left hand seizes downward to the left.

It is almost the same as *Grasping the Sparrow's Tail* on the right side, except the right arm must Ward-Off upwards to the corner.

Retain a light and sensitive energy on top of the head. Hollow the chest and raise the back. Sink the shoulders and suspend the elbows. Relax the waist and coccyx. Keep the spirit of the gaze to the front right side. (See illustration #52.)

Illustration #52 Text
The body is not to be too bent.
The [right] hand is not to be too straight or too high.
The [right] knee is not to pass over the toes.

Applications
1) Proceeding from the use of *Horizontal Single Whip,* if the opponent attacks directly in front of you with his left hand, first arc your left hand to the right to Stick [黏, Nian] to his hand, then sink your right hand to the left as your left hand seizes his hand, stepping your right foot forward and placing it behind his leg. At the same time, send your right arm to the left under his left armpit and attack with a Ward-Off upward to the right.

2) If the opponent backs you off by doing a horizontal rending to your chest with his left arm, you can grab his [left] wrist with your left hand, drawing back your left foot, then step forward with your right foot while sending your right arm under his left armpit, attacking with a Ward-Off to the right and upward.

3) Or the outside of your right forearm Wards-Off to the outside of the opponent's forearm.

61) Wild Horse Parting Its Mane (Left Style)

野馬分鬃 (左式)

Ye Ma Fen Zong (Zuo Shi)

(式左) 鬃分馬野 (53)

From the right style of this posture, the right palm turns over to face downward and circles along with the hips as they settle to the left rear, the left hand circling inward until in front of the chest, the palm turning upward, as the left foot steps diagonally forward to the left.

The knee gradually bends and the left leg becomes substantial, the right leg gradually straightening, as the hands spread apart in unison above and below. It is almost the same as *Grasping the Sparrow's Tail (Left Style)*, but with the left arm

145

Warding-Off upward diagonally to the left while the right hand seizes downward to the right. The rest is the same as in the previous posture. (See Illustration #53.)

Illustration #53 Text
The body is not to lean too much.
The [left] hand is not to be too straightened or too high.
The [left] knee is not to pass over the toes.

Applications
1) Proceeding from the use of the stance on the right side, when the opponent's energy becomes coarse, turn your hips to the right, Pushing aside his right arm with your right hand. Taking advantage of the opportunity to grab his right wrist with your right hand, draw back your right foot and step forward with the left, placing it again behind his leg.

At the same time, send your left arm under his right armpit, attacking with a Ward-Off to the left and upward.

2) If the opponent backs you off by doing a horizontal rending to your chest with his right arm, you can grab his right wrist with your right hand, drawing back your right foot, then step forward with your left foot while sending your left arm under his right armpit, attacking with a Ward-Off to the left and upward.

3) Or the outside of your left forearm Wards-Off to the outside of the opponent's left arm, setting up for continuing into the stance on the right side.

62) Wild Horse Parting Its Mane (Right Style)

野馬分鬃 (右式)

Ye Ma Fen Zong (You Shi)

(式右) 鬃分馬野 (52)

From the left-style stance, the left palm turns over to face downward and circles along with the hips as they settle to the right rear, the right hand circling inward until in front of the chest, the palm turning over to face upward, as the right foot steps out to the right. The rest is the same as in Posture #60.

63) Grasping the Sparrow's Tail (Left Style)
攬雀尾 (左式)
Lan Qiao Wei (Zuo Shi)

（式左）尾雀攬（3）

From the posture of *Wild Horse Parting Its Mane (Right Style)*, the right palm turns over to face downward, circling to the left rear along with the hips, the left hand circling inward until below the right elbow, the palm turned over to face upward. The left foot goes to the left a half step and the hands spread apart to the front and rear, the left forearm going to the left and forward to Ward-Off horizontally. The rest is the same as in Posture #3.

64) Step Forward to Ward-Off, Roll-Back, Press, and Push

上步掤攦擠按

Shang Bu Peng Lu Ji An

掤 （4） 攦 （5）

擠 （6） 按 （7）

See Posture #35.

65) Single Whip

單鞭

Dan Bian

See Posture #8.

66) Jade Maiden Weaves at Shuttles (1)
玉女穿梭 (一)

Yu Nu Chuan Suo (Yi)

（一）梭穿女玉（54）

From the previous *Single Whip* posture, the right hand follows the hips by circling to the left, and as it reaches its full extent, the left hand circles to the right to be in front of the chest, while the body and left toes turn to point to the right corner.

The right foot lifts and takes a half step forward to the right, the right hand going forward and upward, drawing in. The left hand (palm facing upward) goes under the right forearm and Wards-Off upward as the right palm circles upward and withdraws inward until in front of the chest.

The left arm Wards-Off upward until in front of the forehead, turning over so the palm is facing outward as the left foot steps forward to the corner.

Gradually the knee bends and the left leg becomes substantial, the right leg gradually straightening, as the right palm goes from under the left forearm and Pushes forward to the corner.

The right arm should not overly extend. The left knee should not go beyond the toes. Settle the waist and loosen the hips. Tuck in the Tail Gateway. The body should not lean forward. Retain a light and sensitive energy on top of the head. Hollow the chest and raise the back. Sink the shoulders and suspend the elbows. Seat the wrists and straighten the fingers. Keep the gaze forward. (See Illustration #54.)

Illustration #54 Text
The body must not lean forward.
The [left] hand is not to be too straight.
The [left] knee should not pass over the knee.

Applications
1) After using *Single Whip*, the opponent attacks from your right rear with his right hand. Turn around to Neutralize [化, Hua] it by sinking it down with your right hand. If he lifts his hand up, take advantage of the momentum by lifting your left forearm up to Ward-Off his right wrist or elbow, at the same time stepping forward with your right foot, then stepping forward with your left foot, which hooks around his right heel, and Pushing to his chest (or ribs) with your right palm.

2) If the opponent directly in front of you strikes your chest with his right fist, your right hand seizes his right wrist while your right foot presses his right knee (or shin). If he retreats his right leg, take advantage of the opportunity by stepping forward with your right foot, sending your left arm upward to Ward-Off his right arm and striking his chest with your right palm.

67) Jade Maiden Weaves at Shuttles (2)

玉女穿梭 (二)

Yu Nu Chuan Suo (Er)

（二）梭穿女玉（55）

From the previous stance, the left toes turn to the right, the hands going along with the hips by circling to the right, the right hand circling until beside the right ribs then inward and scooping to the left under the left wrist, the hands making an X shape.

The hands continue circling to the right and upward until beside the right side of the forehead and then sink down to the left until in front of the chest, the right foot going to the right rear and taking a half step out to the corner. Gradually the knee bends and the leg becomes substantial, the left leg gradually straightening, the body also having turned around to the right rear, and the right arm Wards-Off upward to the right (the hand in front of the forehead) as the left palm goes from under the right forearm and Pushes forward to the corner. The rest is the same as in the previous posture. (See Illustration #55.)

Illustration #55 Text
The hands are not to be too straight.
The [right] knee is not to pass over the toes.
The body is not to bend forward.

Applications
Proceeding from the first *Jade Maiden Weaves at Shuttles*, the opponent from behind and to your right strikes downward to your head with his right hand. Turn around and Ward-Off with your right forearm, stepping forward with your right foot, and Push to his chest (or ribs) with your left palm.

68) Jade Maiden Weaves at Shuttles (3)
玉女穿梭（三）
Yu Nu Chuan Suo (San)

（三）梭穿女玉（56）

From the previous stance, the hands follow the hips by circling to the left, the right foot lifting and stepping out a half step, the right hand going forward and upward, drawing in. The left foot steps forward to the corner as the right palm circles upward and withdraws until in front of the chest.

The left arm Wards-Off upward as the right palm goes from under the left forearm and Pushes forward to the corner. It is the same as *Jade Maiden Weaves at Shuttles (1)*, just facing a different direction. (See Illustration #56.)

Illustration #56 Text

The [right] hand is not to be too straight.

The [left] knee is not to pass over the toes.

The body is not to bend towards the front.

69) Jade Maiden Weaves at Shuttles (4)
玉女穿梭 (四)
Yu Nu Chuan Suo (Si)

（四）梭穿女玉（57）

Same as *Jade Maiden Weaves at Shuttles (2)*, except facing a different direction. (See Illustration #57.)

Illustration #57 Text
The right hand is like an upwards Ward-Off, but not too high. The left palm is like a Push, but is not held too far forward.

Chen Kung's Note

These four stances each face a different corner. The first is to the southeast, second is to the northeast, third is to the northwest, and fourth is to the southwest.

70) Grasping the Sparrow's Tail (Left Style)
攬雀尾（左式）

Lan Qiao Wei (Zuo Shi)

（式左）尾雀攬（3）

See Posture #63.

71) Step Forward to Ward-Off, Roll-Back, Press, and Push

上步掤攦擠按

Shang Bu Peng Lu Ji An

掤 （4）   攦 （5）

擠 （6）   按 （7）

See Posture #35.

72) Single Whip

單鞭

Dan Bian

See Posture #8.

73) Cloud Hands

雲手

Yun Shou

（一）手雲（31）

（二）手雲（32）　　　（三）手雲（33）

See Posture #37.

74) Single Whip

單鞭

Dan Bian

See Posture #8.

75) Snake Lowering Its Body

蛇身下勢

She Shen Xia Shi

勢下身蛇 (58)

Proceeding from *Single Whip,* as the hips move back follow
them with the hands, creating a half-circle shape from up
to down, until the left hand is drawn back to the front of
the chest. (The left arm is bent, while the right arm remains
unmoved from the previous stance.)

At the same time, squat down bending the right leg,
shifting the weight to it, and straightening the left leg. Bring
the left hand down again (until it is in front of the abdomen),

and stretch it out forward. (See Illustration #58.) Do not lean forward too much, and keep the eyes on the hand.

Illustration #58 Text
The body should not lean to the front.
The [right] hand should not be held too high or too low.
The [right] knee is not to be too far outwards.

Applications
1) Proceeding from the use of *Single Whip*, if the opponent attacks with his right hand, grasp his wrist with your left hand and pluck it down. If he braces it upward, take advantage of his strength by using your right hand to deflect it upwards; then, use the palm or fist of your left hand to strike his crotch.

2) If the opponent attacks with his right hand, grasp it with your left hand to sink it down. If he then attacks your right temple with a diagonal strike using his left hand, use your right hand to borrow [借勁, Jie Jing, Borrowing Energy] the momentum and sink it down. Now both his hands are restrained, so he will surely attempt to kick your crotch with his right foot; squat down, take the opportunity to scoop under his heel with your left hand and lift slightly upward. Push the sole of his foot with your right hand as you lift your body, using both hands to propel him out.

76) Golden Rooster Stands On One Leg (Right Style)

金雞獨立 (右 式)

Jin Ji Du Li (You Shi)

（式右）立獨鷄金（59）

Proceeding from the posture of *Snake Lowering Its Body*, turn the left toes across to the left, moving the body forward; lift the right foot and step forward, toes touching down, heel lifted, making an Empty Stance with the weight on the left leg. (The right foot can also stay lifted from the ground.)

Follow the right leg forward with the right hand until it is next to the right side of the waist; it then makes a circle going back and to the right. Sink the shoulders and relax the waist,

167

gradually raising it up following the rise of the body, fingers upward. Bend and lift the right knee, toes hanging down slightly, the right elbow and knee aligned with each other above and below, the left palm pushing down (fingers extended forward, palm facing downward) until it is next to the left thigh. (See Illustration #59.)

Keep the head up without tension. Draw back the chest and straighten the back. The hand should not go too high. The body should not rise too far. The elbow and knee should be aligned with each other. Keep the gaze forward.

Illustration #59 Text
The spirit of the eyes gazes at the [right] hand.
Retain a light and sensitive energy on top of the head.
Hollow the chest and raise the back.

Applications
1) Proceeding from the use of *Snake Lowering Its Body,* if the opponent retreats and attacks from above with his left hand, take advantage of the opportunity by sending your body forward and lifting upward, seizing his left hand with your right as your right knee strikes his lower abdomen.

2) If the opponent attacks from above with his right hand, Ward-Off upward with your right hand and bring your left hand upward from under your right forearm to drive his right hand clear. Then, strike across to his head with the back of your right hand, which he will have to use his left hand to deal [block] with. Take advantage of this and using your hands to spread his hands apart while attacking his groin with your right knee. If he Neutralizes [化, Hua] this by drawing back

and plucking your hands with his, use a toe kick (or pressing kick).

3) If the opponent attacks with his right hand, grab his wrist with your left hand and feign an attack to his face with your right hand that he will have to deal with using his left hand; then take advantage of this by spreading his hands and kneeing his crotch. As he draws back, kick (or stomp) him with your right foot.

77) Golden Rooster Stands On One Leg (Left Style)
金雞獨立（左式）

Jin Ji Du Li (Zuo Shi)

（式左）立獨鷄金（60）

From the previous posture, bring the right foot down and squat down slightly while lowering the right hand until it is next to the right hip (fingers extended forward, palm facing down). The left hand makes a circle toward the left and rear, shoulder sinking and waist loosening, and gradually follows the body upwards, fingers upward. At the same time, bend and raise the left knee, toes hanging down slightly (the weight on the right leg).

The left elbow and knee should be aligned with each other, above and below. (See Illustration #60.) The rest is the same as in the previous posture.

Illustration #60 Text
The [left] hand is not to be held too high.
[The left] elbow and knee unite.
The body should not lean too much.

Applications
1) Proceeding from the use of the right stance, if the opponent Neutralizes [化, Hua] your right knee by sinking it down with his left hand, attacking with his right hand, follow him by bringing your right leg down and brushing his left hand down with your right hand; seize his right hand with your left while striking his groin with your left knee.

For 2 & 3, see the previous posture, but left and right hands and feet are reversed.

78) Moving Backwards to Chase the Monkey Away

倒撐猴

Tao Nian Hou

Proceeding from the previous *Golden Rooster Standing On One Leg*, take a half step back with the left foot, steadying the body as it comes down. The left palm goes forward with a sinking Push and then Pulls Back (with the palm facing upward), the right leg becoming insubstantial. Follow the movement with the right palm by circling it around to the rear and upward until it is next to the right ear, then Push forward with it as the left palm Pulls Back next to the left hip. The rest is the same as in Postures #25 & #26.

（式右）猴撐倒（23）　　　（式左）猴撐倒（24）

79) Diagonal Flying Posture

斜飛勢

Xie Fei Shi

勢 飛 斜 (25)

See Posture #27.

80) Lifting Hands Posture
提手上勢
Ti Shou Shang Shi

（9）提手上勢

See Posture #9.

81) White Crane Cooling Its Wings

白鶴涼翅

Bai He Liang Chi

翅涼鶴白（10）

See Posture #10.

82) Brush the Knee and Twist Step

摟膝拗步

Lou Xi Ao Bu

（11）摟膝拗步（左式）

See Posture #11.

83) Needle at Sea Bottom

海底針

Hai Di Zhen

針 底 海 (26)

See Posture #31.

84) Fan Penetrates the Back

扇通背

Shan Tong Bei

背 通 扇 （27）

See Posture #32.

85) Turn Body, White Snake Spits Out Tongue
轉身白蛇吐信

Zhuan Shen Bai She Tu Xin

信吐蛇白身轉（61）

Proceeding from *Fan Penetrates the Back*, shift the left toes inward to the right, the right palm going upward as the waist turns to the rear. Lift the right foot and bring it down ahead and to the side (the body now completely turned around from the previous stance), drawing back the right palm (palm upward) until it is next to the right ribs and forms a fist; the left elbow follows the turning of the hips by rolling until in front of the chest.

The left palm strikes forward in front of the chest, with the palm (facing outward) as the right fist extends forward, becoming a palm (facing upwards), the fingers jabbing forward like a white snake flicking out its tongue. (See Illustration #61.)

Sink the shoulders and suspend the elbows. Relax the waist and coccyx. Keep the gaze forward.

Illustration #61 Text
The body is not to lean too much.
The left palm maintains a Sinking Energy [沉 勁, Chen Jin].

Applications
Same as *Swipe Across the Body and Chop*, except using your right fingers as though flicking something away in order to jab to the opponent's solar plexus or ribs. This posture expresses with fierceness, and so if you are not an expert at applying it, you should not attempt to use it, otherwise you may injure someone, which is why instructors are often reluctant to freely explain its function.

Chen Kung's Note
Nowadays most practitioners simply replace this posture with *Swipe Across the Body and Chop* because turning around makes it difficult to practice.

86) Step Forward, Remove, Parry, and Punch

進步搬攔捶

Jin Bu Ban Lan Chui

捶 （17）

See Posture #19 [or Posture #34 and illustration #30].

87) Step Forward to Ward-Off, Roll-Back, Press, and Push

上步掤攦擠按

Shang Bu Peng Lu Ji An

前視神眼 勁頂頜虛
身勿前俯
稍屈勿太高
手臂宜
膝勿伸
過足尖

掤（4）

太短
勁不易出
過長
勁易斷

攦（5）

過高
上身易
出而不沉肩

擠（6）

太出
勁易鬆

按（7）

See Posture #35.

88) Single Whip

單鞭

Dan Bian

See Posture #8.

89) Cloud Hands

雲手

Yun Shou

（一）手雲（31）

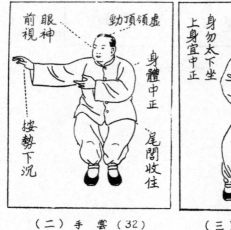

（二）手雲（32）

（三）手雲（33）

See Posture #37.

90) Single Whip
單鞭

Dan Bian

See Posture #8.

91) High Pat on Horse

高採馬

Gao Cai Ma

馬採高 (34)

See Posture #39.

92) Crossing Hands

十字手

Shi Zi Shou

手 字 十 (62)

Proceeding from the posture of *High Pat On Horse*, thread the left hand (palm upward) over the right arm (near the back of the wrist) and extending it forward as the left foot takes a half step forward.

Bend the left knee, the right leg following the stance by straightening forward (making a Bow Stance with the legs). The right hand follows the stance by drawing back until it is in front of the chest, the back of the wrist beneath the left arm. (See Illustration #62.)

187

The left arm should not be too straight. The body should not lean forward. Keep the gaze ahead.

Illustration #62 Text
The [left] arm is not to be too straightened.
The body is not to lean to the front.

Applications
1) Proceeding from the use of *High Pat On Horse,* after your right palm has struck the opponent's face, lift his left arm upward [with your left arm] and then sink it downwards to the rear with your right arm to Neutralize [化, Hua] his left arm, and send your left palm threading over your right arm with a finger jab [thrust] to his throat.

2) Press down the opponent's hand with your right hand as your left thrusts to his throat (or solar plexus).

93) Turn Body to Cross Legs

轉身十字腿

Zhuan Shen Shi Zi Tui

腿字十身轉（63）

Proceeding from the previous *Crossing Hands*, the left toes follow the body as it turns to the right; both hands form a slanted cross-shape (the right hand turns within the left, remaining within the slanted cross-shape).

Lift the right foot and push out forward with the entire sole, spreading the hands apart to both sides at shoulder level. (See Illustration #63.)

The arms should be level with each other. Keep the gaze forward.

Illustration #63 Text

Sink the shoulders and suspend the elbows.
The body is not to lean back.
The two arms are on line.
The [bottom of the right] foot kicks outwards.

Applications

See Posture #42.

Chen Kung's Note

In the old Tai Ji Quan form, the *Crossing Legs* kicking method was to lift the right leg and press forward with the sole after the body had turned and the hands arced to the right side. However, then the hands instead spread apart at shoulder level with the left hand going forward and the right hand to the rear. This version is very effective, it is not easy to practice without skill in the waist and legs. For this reason, nowadays most people perform it as described above.

94) Brush the Knee and Direct Punch to Groin

摟膝指襠捶

Lou Xi Zhi Dang Chui

捶襠指膝摟（64）

Proceeding from *Turn Body to Cross Legs,* bring the right foot down forward, both hands following the hips as they turn to the right. Shift the right toes across to the right (becoming firm). Follow the hips with the right hand by making a circle outwards to the right, forming a fist (Tiger's Mouth facing up). Place it beside the right hip while the left hand follows the waist by circling to the right until it is in front of the chest. Step forward and out with the left foot, gradually bending the knee and squatting down, brushing downward past the left knee with the left hand and then placing it beside the left hip. At the same time, strike diagonally forward with the right fist (the Tiger's Mouth upward; this is different from *Advance Step to Plant Punch* because the *Direct Punch to Groin* strikes forward while *Planting Fist* is downward). The right leg follows the stance by straightening gradually. (See Illustration #64.)

Lean forward slightly, but not too far. When you send out the right fist, the arc should be more forward than downward. Relax the waist and coccyx. Hollow the chest and raise the back. Keep the gaze forward.

Illustration #64 Text
The body is not to bend over too much.
The spirit of the eyes gazes at the fist.
The right fist is directed on an arc line, and is not directed
    towards the ground.

Applications
See Posture #44, except now striking the crotch.

95) Step Forward to Ward-Off, Roll-Back, Press, and Push

上步掤攦擠按

Shang Bu Peng Lu Ji An

掤 （4）　　　　攦 （5）

擠 （6）　　　　按 （7）

Proceeding from *Brush the Knee and Direct Punch to the Groin,*
bring the hands down to follow the waist and legs as they
turn to the left. At the same time, move and turn the left toes
across and to the left (becoming substantial); step forward
with the right foot while both hands go forward and upward
to make a Ward-Off gesture. The rest is the same as in
Postures #4–7.

96) Single Whip

單鞭

Dan Bian

See Posture #8.

97) Snake Lowering Its Body
蛇身下勢

She Shen Xia Shi

勢下身蛇（58）

See Posture #75.

98) Step Forward to Seven Star

上步七星

Shang Bu Qi Xing

眼神前視

身勿前俯

尾閭中正

星七步上（65）

From the previous posture, *Snake Lowering Its Body,* shift the left toes across and to the left, moving the body forward and upward; rise gradually as the weight shifts to the left leg. Make a fist with the left hand and place it in front of the chest; also make a fist with the right hand and strike forward (Tiger's Mouth facing upward) under the left wrist. At the same time the right foot follows the right fist and kicks out forward with the toes without touching the ground.

Retain a light and sensitive energy on top of the head. Hollow the chest and raise the back. The body should not lean forward. Center the Tail Gateway and keep the gaze forward. (See Illustration #65.)

Illustration #65 Text
The spirit of the eyes gazes to the front.
The body is not to bend forward.
The Tail Gateway is to be centered and upright.

Applications
1) Proceeding from the use of *Snake Lowering Its Body,* if the opponent strikes with his right hand, rise up and use crossed fists to Ward-Off forward and upward; at the same time, use your right foot to kick his lower body. Or, strike his solar plexus with your right fist while kicking with your right foot as you make an upper frame with your left fist.

2) If the opponent strikes with his right hand, divert it to the left with your left hand to weaken it. At the same time, feint to his chest with your right fist; he will need to use his left hand to block it, at which point you can take advantage of the situation by kicking his lower body with your right foot.

3) You can draw in the opponent's right fist with your left hand, then attack from above and below with your right fist and right foot.

99) Retreat Step to Ride the Tiger
退步跨虎

Tui Bu Kua Hu

虎 跨 步 退 （66）

Proceeding from *Step Forward to Seven Star*, take half a step
back with the right foot, steadying the body as it comes down;
spread the hands apart upward and downward.

Relax the waist and coccyx and squat down. Just as in
White Crane Cooling Its Wings, kick out forward with the left
foot, entering an Empty Stance as it comes down; the toes
touch the ground and the heel is lifted.

Retain a light and sensitive energy on top of the head. Hollow the chest and raise the back. Keep the spirit of the gaze to the front. (See Illustration #66.)

Illustration #66 Text
Both hands are mutually opposite, divided openly and
    separated.
The left foot is in an Insubstantial Stance.
Hollow the chest and raise the back.

Applications
Proceeding from the use of *Step Forward to Seven Star,* if the opponent tries to seize your right hand down, because you cannot kick high with your right foot, you can follow the stance and bring your right foot down. Relax the waist and coccyx, and spread your hands apart, kicking his lower body with your left foot.

100) Turn Body to Sweep the Lotus Blossoms
轉身擺蓮
Zhuan Shen Bai Lian

蓮擺身轉（67）

Proceeding from *Retreat Step to Ride the Tiger,* bring the right hand under the left and then make a three-dimensional circle by going upwards and to the left. At the same time, the left hand goes upwards and to the left and then makes a three-dimensional circle by going downwards and to the right.

Clasp the two hands together, left palm scooping under the right armpit (palm facing downward), right hand rising upward (palm facing inward). The left foot is suspended, and the right heel lifts so the ball of the foot touches the ground.

Turn the body to the right, the hands following the turn by brushing downward; after turning back to the starting position, both of the feet should be on the ground, with the weight now on the left leg and the right foot making an Empty Stance with the heel slightly lifted.

Squat down, the hands sinking down until they are beside the right thigh; they then spread about a foot apart to the sides (palms facing downward), following the hips and going upward to the left, circling around to the right. Once the hands are by the right side of the forehead, lift the right foot upwards and to the left, then swing it to the right. The back of the foot sweeps across, and you slap it with the palms. (See Illustration #67.)

Illustration #67 Text
The upper body must be centered and upright.

Applications
1) Proceeding from the use of a Seated Tiger Stance [also called Crouching Tiger Stance], Withdraw Step and seize the opponent's right wrist with your right hand and scoop your left hand over your right forearm to strike diagonally forward at his face with your palm. If he rushes forward to attack, dodge away by spinning to the right; once you have spun all the way around, seize his right hand with your right hand and use the edge of your right foot to kick his right ribs (or waist). This is a means of snatching victory from defeat. It is not easy, but if you are able to perform it successfully, you are both skillful as well as courageous.

2) If the opponent strikes your chest with his right hand, seize his hand with your right hand and use the edge of your right foot to kick across at his ribs or waist.

101) Bend Bow to Shoot the Tiger

彎弓射虎

Wan Gong She Hu

虎射·弓彎 (68)

Proceeding from the previous posture, *Turn Body to Sweep the Lotus Blossoms,* bring the right foot down firmly ahead and to the right, the hands becoming fists and following the hips by circling back and to the right; the left fist circles until it is in front of the chest, the right fist until it is below and to the right of the jaw.

Relax the waist and coccyx, as well as hollow the chest and raise the back. Then squat down and extend the fists

toward the left corner, Tiger's Mouths facing each other.
(See Illustration #68.)

Retain a light and sensitive energy on top of the head
and do not let the body lean too far or let the left arm
straighten too much. The fists should be loose and the
gaze on the left corner.

Illustration #68 Text

The [right] fist is not to be grasped tightly.
The [left] arm is not to be too straightened.
The body is not to bend too much.

Applications

1) Proceeding from the use of *Turn Body to Sweep the
Lotus Blossoms*, if the opponent retreats to weaken you,
Stick [黏, Nian] to his hand with your hands, sink into
an arc to the right, and then strike him with double fists.

2) If the opponent strikes your chest with his right hand,
hook his right wrist with your right hand and Push his right
shoulder with your left hand as you turn your body to the
right. Take advantage of the opportunity and lift up to seize
him, causing him to lose his balance so you can Push out
with both hands. If his left hand comes out to meet your
right hand, your hands can use power from your hips to
weaken him and turn, striking his chest.

102) Swipe Across the Body and Chop

撇身捶

Pie Shen Chui

捶 身 撇 (14)

Proceeding from *Bend Bow to Shoot the Tiger*, shift the left toes across to the left while forming a palm with the right hand and striking forward; the left hand also becomes a palm under the right arm, then both hands lower and arc back and to the left. Lift the right foot and take a half step across and forward to make the *Swipe Across the Body and Chop* posture. The remainder is the same as Posture #18.

103) Step Forward, Remove, Parry, and Punch
進步搬攔捶

Jin Bu Ban Lan Chui

捶 （17）

See Posture #19.

104) Sealing to Appear As Closing
如封似閉

Ru Feng Si Bi

閉似封如 (18)

See Posture #20.

105) Conclusion of Tai Ji

合太極

He Tai Ji

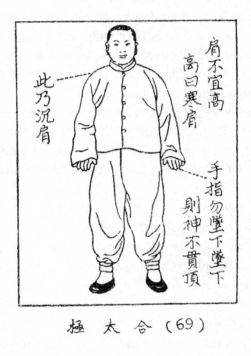

極 太 合 （69）

From the previous posture, turn the body to the right, shifting the left toes inward to the right until they are parallel with the right foot. The hands go upward and spread apart, palms facing outward and arcing downward as the body squats down (as though embracing and lifting something), then coming upward and together to form a cross-shape (as in the first part of Posture #21), palms inward and Warding-Off upward to chest level. (When Warding-Off, relax the waist and coccyx.)

At the same time lift the right foot and take a half step inward to the left, both hands hanging down, palms downward, fingers extended forward. This is the same as the *Beginning Tai Ji Quan Posture.* (See Illustration #69.)

Retain a light and sensitive energy and let the breath sink into the lower abdomen to gather the Qi and concentrate the spirit. Stop and stand for a time to allow the Qi and blood to return to their original condition.

(Conclusion of Tai Ji should return to the same position as the *Beginning Tai Ji Quan posture.* If desiring this, match the distance by performing *Cloud Hands* the same number of times as *Moving Backwards to Chase the Monkey Away.)*

Illustration #69 Text
The arms are not to be straight or high.
The fingers are not to be collapsed downwards, doing so
    results in the spirit not being able to penetrate to the
    top of the head.

Chen Kung's Note
The purpose of this text is to make things easier for students to understand and learn; therefore, the large frame Tai Ji Quan is provided in the explanations above so beginners may benefit from the experience of others. As for the middle and small frames, their essentials cannot be adequately explained in writing here because each posture contains many circles and requires precise executions; for this reason, this book has not attempted to present them.[1]

Translator's Note

1. *Frames* are determined by the expansiveness of performing a particular movement. Chen Kung says the explanations in this book apply to the *Large Frame*. As one becomes more proficient, the movements of the postures become more compact and precise. The idea here is that initially a practitioner needs an expansive expression of energy to perform the postures and their applications, but over time the energy can be issued with smaller, rather than larger, circles. The highest level, *Small Frame,* occurs when the circling and issuing of energy cannot be seen by others.

Appendix

The following excerpts (verses and commentaries) come from *Tai Ji Quan Treatise* (Daoist Immortal Three Peaks Zhang Series) by Stuart Alve Olson, published by Valley Spirit Arts. The *Tai Ji Quan Treatise* is attributed to Zhang Sanfeng, founder of Taijiquan.

Verse from the Tai Ji Quan Treatise

太極拳論

Tai Ji Quan Lun

Calmly stimulate the Qi, so the spirit is retained internally.

氣宜鼓盪. 神宜內斂.

Qi yi gu dang. Shen yi nei lian.

Moving water cannot be boiled is the underlying message of "calmly stimulate the Qi." The Qi is like an inherent oxygen within the blood deriving its power in the same manner as steam coming off boiling water.

Actually, the very ideogram for Qi in the Chinese shows a pot with rice inside being cooked, with the vapors rising and symbolizing the energy of Qi. In the human body, the idea is the same. The lower abdomen is like the pot, the breath like the fire, and the lower Elixir Field[3] the rice. When we keep our breath in

---

3   See note 11, p. 24.

the lower abdomen, the fluids in the stomach are heated, and this stimulates the Elixir Field to expand. Like the pot in which the rice is cooked, it must remain undisturbed over the fire in order to cook. Hence, to stimulate the Qi in the abdomen, it must be done calmly and without forcing the breath.

To give a better understanding of this principle, use a visualization technique by imagining a pot of water within your abdomen, filled to the brim, and then move through the Taijiquan postures with utmost concentration so as not to spill one drop of water from the pot—making no jerking-like motions, no disconnected movements, no leaning, and no sporadic movements.

In this way the Qi can be calmly stimulated and the mind-intent fully placed in the lower Elixir Field.

The Chinese character for Qi means two things: "breath" and "energy." Energy here means the very source of what animates a human body. Qi is the energy that allows motion in a human being. Therefore, the more powerful the breath is the greater the energy of the body will be, and the more natural the movement and animation of the body will be. For example, a common trick or game you may have played as a child involves standing in a doorway and pressing your hands against the door jambs with great force. If you have ever tried this, you know that when you release your hands from the door, the arms will float upward all by themselves. This is one of the best examples of how the Qi animates the body.

From creating tension in the arms, you are blocking the Qi and blood flow. When you release the pressure on the door jams, the blood and Qi rapidly rush back into the arms, creating a movement that is not generated by external muscular force. It is precisely this sensation people should feel in their hands and arms throughout their Taijiquan form practice. If not, then it really isn't Taijiquan. When the arms feel as if they are floating, the Qi is being calmly stimulated.

Another example demonstrating the idea of calmly stimulating the Qi is to stand upright with the hands held in front of the thighs, elbows slightly bent, and the shoulders dropped and released of all tension. Focus all your attention into the lower Elixir Field and simply breathe. This will cause the hands and arms to gradually float and sink according to the breath. After some practice with this exercise, the hands and arms will naturally float up to shoulder level when the breathing is full and strong. In essence, it's a measure of how strong your Qi is.

When about to start performing any Taijiquan form, stand first and just breathe. Let the hands and arms rise and fall according to the breath. This is exactly what is meant by letting the mind first lead the Qi, the Qi will then lead the blood, and the blood will lead the body. Place all the attention into the lower Elixir Field, then the breath and Qi will follow and generate from there. At this point, the Qi mobilizes the blood circulation throughout the entire body, and this causes the body to be capable of creating motion without external muscular force.

To *calmly stimulate the Qi,* you must first put all your attention into the lower Elixir Field, and this is where the second part of this verse comes in, "so the spirit is retained internally." Actually, this verse could also read, "When the spirit is retained internally, the Qi can be calmly stimulated," as each stimulates the other.

The meaning of "so the spirit is retained internally" is really defined by the idea of mind-intention. Meaning, when fully focusing on the abdomen, or better said, "abiding by the lower Elixir Field," the breath and Qi will begin to generate and accumulate there. Just like with infants, it is not only their abdomen that moves with the breath, but their entire body.

Infants are still generating breath from where the umbilical cord was attached, and over time, as we age, the breath will rise into the lungs. As Taoists say, "the spirit [mind-intention] begins to rise toward the head."

In Taijiquan, the idea is to reverse this process, so the breath (Qi) is led back down into the lower abdomen, where it is with infants. *Abiding by the lower Elixir Field,* then, sensing and focusing on the lower abdomen, is the essence of internally retaining the spirit. When breathing in this way, the Qi will likewise be calmly stimulated.

In *The Mental Elucidation of the Thirteen Kinetic Operations* by Wang Zongyue, it is said,

Your mind-intention must be focused on retaining the spirit internally, not on the breath and Qi.

If your mind focuses only on the breath and Qi, the result will be stagnation; you will only have breath, but no strength of the Qi.

This passage raises the question on how to breathe while performing the Taijiquan movements. As Master Liang would say, "Don't worry, by and by you will know it."

This simple answer was not his attempt to avoid the question, but to get a student to let it happen naturally. Just put your attention into the lower Elixir Field and abide by it. Sensing the lower abdomen, instead of trying to make something happen there, allows the Qi to sink naturally into it. No one can force the Qi into the lower Elixir Field; it must be done naturally and with mind-intent.

"Sink" is an important word choice, because it implies no force or expansion of the breath to get the Qi into the lower Elixir Field, just mind-intent and allowing it to sink downward.

The bigger question pertaining to this verse is why you need to *calmly stimulate the Qi* and *retain the spirit internally?* Actually, these functions are at the root of mastering all Taijiquan skills—and occur from abiding by the lower Elixir Field.

To develop the Qi, it must first be stimulated calmly. This calm stimulation has its source in the lower Elixir Field. The Qi is calmly mobilized through the circulation of the breath and blood, and the source of doing this is through the mind-intent.

From abiding by the lower Elixir Field, the Qi, breath, and blood begin circulating more fully throughout the entire body and, consequently, are heated. This internal heat then starts affecting the sinews, tendons, and muscles of the body. Once the warm Qi, breath, and blood have entered the muscles, they begin to penetrate into the bones and help create more marrow, thus increasing pliability of the bones and leading to greater health.

When the Qi circulates freely throughout the body, it can then be directed through the arms and into the hands. This is the true nurturing of Qi and it originates with the mind-intent.

Therefore, to retain the spirit internally is actually rooted in the principle of sinking the Qi into the lower Elixir Field.

The second benefit from abiding by the lower Elixir Field can be seen in the self-defense aspects because all the responses will be directed by the waist rather than by the upper body. And, because the reactionary force is generated from the waist, the Qi and Jin (intrinsic energy) can be more easily expressed as well.

Intrinsic energy comes from the sinews and tendons, and so the more pliable and stronger they are, the greater the energy that can be released. When the Qi and Jin are expressed together, nothing is stronger. Therefore, this verse, "Calmly stimulate the Qi, so the spirit is retained internally," is full of meaning and purpose and is essential to the correct practice of Taijiquan.

The Foundational Principles of Tai Ji Quan

太 極 拳 基 本 要 點

Tai Ji Quan Ji Ben Yao Dian

First presented in Chen Kung's book *Tai Ji Quan, Sword, Saber, Staff, and Dispersing Hands Combined,* the following list consolidates the theories of principles for the correct practice of Taijiquan. Chen Kung derived the list of these principles from the Yang family transcripts and they have become a standard reference for all Taijiquan forms. Master Liang always stressed teaching principles as the essence and heart of Taijiquan practice. Someone may learn the movements correctly from a teacher, but without the mastery of the underlying principles, the full skills and benefits of Taijiquan practice can never be accomplished. All practitioners of Taijiquan should deeply study and apply these principles to their practice so they can master the art of Taijiquan in its fullest sense.

1) Retain a light and sensitive energy on top of the head.

一) 虛 領 頂 勁.

Yi) Xu ling ding jin.

2) Express the spirit in the eyes to concentrate the gaze.

二) 眼 神 注 視.

Er) Yan shen zhu shi.

3) Hollow the chest and raise the back.

三) 含胸拔背.

San) Han Xiong Ba Bei.

4) Sink the shoulders and suspend the elbows.

四) 沈肩垂肘.

Si) Chen jian chui zhou.

5) Seat the wrist and straighten the fingers.

五) 坐腕伸指.

Wu) Zuo Wan Shen Zhi.

6) Keep the entire body centered and upright.

六) 身體中正.

Liu) Shen ti zhong zheng.

7) Draw in the Tail Gateway.

七) 尾闾收住.

Qi) Wei Lu shou zhu.

8) Relax the waist and relax the coccyx.

八) 鬆腰鬆胯.

Ba) Song yao song kua.

9) The knees appear relaxed, but not so relaxed.

九) 膝部如鬆無鬆.

Jiu) Xi bu ru song wu song.

10) Adhere the soles of the feet to the ground.

十) 足掌貼地.

Shi) Zu zhang tie di.

11) Clearly distinguish the insubstantial and substantial.

十一) 分清虛實.

Shi yi) Fen qing xu shi.

12) Upper and lower should mutually follow each other, and the body should move as one unit.

十二) 上下相隨. 週身一致.

Shi er) Shang xia xiang sui. Zhou shen yi zhi.

13) The internal and external should be mutually joined together with natural breathing.

十三) 內外相合. 呼吸自然.

Shi san) Nei wai xiang he. Hu xi zi ran.

14) Use the mind-intent, do not use muscular force.

十四) 用意不用力.

Shi si) Yong yi bu yong li.

15) The Qi should circulate freely throughout the body, yet dividing the upper and lower activity.

十五) 氣遍週身. 分行上下.

Shi wu) Qi bian zhou shen. Fen xing shang xia.

16) Mutually connect the mind-intent and Qi.

十六) 意氣相連.

Shi liu) Yi qi xiang lian.

17) Move in accordance with the gestures of the posture. Do not bend forward and do not expose your back.

十七) 式式势順. 不拗不背. 週身舒適.

Shi qi) Shi shi shi shun. Bu ao bu bei. Zhou shen shu shi.

18) All the gestures are to be uniform, continuous, and unbroken.

十八) 式式均勻. 綿綿不斷.

Shi ba) Shi shi jun yun. Mian mian bu duan.

19) In performing the postures, be free of excess and deficiency, and seek to be centered and upright.

十九) 姿势無過或不及. 當求其中正.

Shi jiu) Zi shi wu guo huo bu ji. Dang qiu ji zong zheng.

20) Use the method of concealing by not outwardly exposing.

二十) 用法含而不露.

Er shi) Yong fa han er bu lu.

21) Seek tranquility within movement; seek movement within tranquility.

二十一) 動中求靜. 靜中求動.

Er shi yi) Dong zhong qiu jing. Jing zhong qiu dong.

22) Lightness brings about nimbleness, nimbleness results in movement, and movement results in transformation.

二十二) 輕則靈. 靈則動. 動則變.

Er shi er) Qing ze ling. Ling ze dong. Dong ze bian.

Think of the first ten *Tai Ji Quan Principles of Movement* as a beginner's guide to applying Taijiquan, and the full twenty-two as more for those who are well acquainted with Taijiquan practice and principles. When these following ten principles [according to Yang Chengfu's view, which varies slightly in order from the previous list] are all applied within each posture and gesture of Taijiquan, all the parts will be strung together so that the entire body can move as one unit.

1. *Suspend the head as if by a thread* means to imagine a light and sensitive energy on top of the head, or to imagine a thread is suspending the head from above. This both stimulates the spirit and keeps the head in perfect alignment.

2. *Concentrate the line of vision* means to move the head and waist in perfect unison as if the eyes were in the waist. This also keeps the spirit focused and keeps the whole body moving as one unit.

3. *Sink the shoulders, suspend the elbows, seat the wrists, and relax the fingers. Sinking the shoulders* means to let them drop naturally, not forcing them down. This is to help keep the breath and Qi from rising into the upper body. *Suspending the elbows* means to imagine they are held in a position to better enable blood circulation and so not to let them collapse into the body. *Seating the wrists* is to imagine as if the hands and wrists were resting on a pillow, so that the wrists and hands are in perfect alignment. This will create the perfect conditions for

blood and Qi to flow freely into the hands. *Relaxing the fingers* means to keep each finger slightly bent, not straight and not curled, so the blood and Qi can enter the fingertips. This entire principle is primarily employed to allow blood and Qi to flow through the entire arm and into the fingertips, as well as to create the conditions for intrinsic energy (jin) to be expressed out through the arms and hands.

4. *Hollow the chest and raise the back* aids in the development of adhering Qi to the spine (raising the back) and sinking the Qi into the lower Elixir Field (hollowing the chest). But it also helps in keeping the back rounded out and sinking the shoulders so that there is no pinching of the shoulder blades together.

5. *Abide by the lower Elixir Field* has two important functions: First, it keeps all the movements generating and functioning from the waist. Second, it keeps the mind-intention on sinking the Qi into the lower Elixir Field.

6. *Draw in the Tail Gateway (tailbone)* keeps the spine aligned and prevents leaning. Drawing in means to tuck the tailbone in and down about one inch so there is no protrusion of the buttocks.

7. *Relax the waist and thighs* means not to collapse the hips inward nor expand them outward, but to keep them in perfect alignment with the thighs. Relaxing the coccyx

opens the perineum area so that blood and Qi can flow into it freely and unobstructed.

8. *Do not let the knee pass over the toes* does not mean the knees can be aligned directly with the toes. It means that the calf and shin of the forward leg is held upright and perpendicular to the floor, so that if looking down the toes can still be seen—as the knee isn't passing over or hiding them. This principle prevents overextension of the legs and from creating too much stress and tension upon the knees and legs.

9. *Round out the legs and knees* is crucial for ridding the legs of tension, for opening up the perineum area, and for developing root (central equilibrium). In all related Asian inner-cultivation methods, be it meditation, yoga, martial art, Taijquan, and so forth, there is this principle of opening the legs so as to allow blood and Qi to enter into the perineum area.

10. *Sink the weight into the Bubbling Well points* on the bottom of the feet is really a misnomer. Actually, it is impossible to place the entire weight of the body into specific Qi centers, especially the Bubbling Well points, as they are located behind the balls of the feet in the hollow area near the center of each foot. Therefore, this principle can't be taken literally. The idea here is that if a person focuses on the Bubbling Well point when committing weight into a given leg, the entire foot can be relaxed and the weight will evenly distribute

throughout the foot. Otherwise, there will be a tendency to press down the foot (causing the root to be easily severed from the tension) or more weight gets placed onto the heel of the foot or into the toes (again causing easy severing of the root).

Applying these ten *Tai Ji Quan Principles of Movement* can be seen, in analogy, as if a person were floating in mid air—from the head being suspended upward and the feet sunk downward—so that the entire body can function freely without hindrance, while the waist controls and generates all function of movement from the body's center.

About the Translator

Stuart Alve Olson, longtime protégé of Master T.T. Liang (1900–2002), is a world renowned teacher, translator, and writer on Taoist philosophy, health, martial art, and internal arts. Since his early twenties, he has studied and practiced Taoism, Chinese Buddhism, and Asian related arts.

As of 2017, Stuart has published more than thirty books, many of which now appear in several foreign-language editions.

Taoist Works

- *Actions & Retributions: A Taoist Treatise on Attaining Spiritual Virtue, Longevity, and Immortality,* Attributed to Lao Zi (Valley Spirit Arts, 2015).
- *Being Daoist: The Way of Drifting with the Current, Revised Edition* (Valley Spirit Arts, 2014).
- *Book of Sun and Moon (I Ching),* volumes I and II (Valley Spirit Arts, 2014).
- *Chen Tuan's Four Season Internal Kungfu* (Valley Spirit Arts, 2016).
- *Clarity & Tranquility: A Guide for Daoist Meditation* (Valley Spirit Arts, 2015).
- *Daoist Sexual Arts: A Guide for Attaining Health, Youthfulness, Vitality, and Awakening the Spirit* (Valley Spirit Arts, 2015).
- *Embryonic Breathing: The Taoist Method of Opening the Dan Tian* (Valley Spirit Arts, 2016).

- *The Immortal: True Accounts of the 250-Year-Old Man, Li Qingyun* by Yang Sen (Valley Spirit Arts, 2014).
- *The Jade Emperor's Mind Seal Classic: The Taoist Guide to Health, Longevity, and Immortality* (Inner Traditions, 2003).
- *Li Qingyun: Longevity Methods of a 250-Year-Old Taoist Immortal* (Valley Spirit Arts, 2016)
- *Qigong Teachings of a Taoist Immortal: The Eight Essential Exercises of Master Li Ching-Yun* (Healing Arts Press, 2002).
- *Refining the Elixir: The Internal Alchemy Teachings of Taoist Immortal Zhang Sanfeng* (Valley Spirit Arts, 2016).
- *The Seen and Unseen: A Taoist Guide for the Meditation Practice of Inner Contemplation* (Valley Spirit Arts, 2016).
- *Tao of No Stress: Three Simple Paths* (Healing Arts Press, 2002).
- *Taoist Chanting & Recitation: At-Home Cultivator's Practice Guide* (Valley Spirit Arts, 2015).
- *Yellow Court: The Exalted One's Scripture on the External Illumination of the Yellow Court,* vol. 1 (Valley Spirit Arts, 2017).
- *Yellow Court: The Highest Clarity Yellow Court Internal Illumination Scripture (Composed by Madame Wei Huacun),* vol. 2 (Valley Spirit Arts, 2017).

Taijiquan Books
Chen Kung Series

- *Tai Ji Qi: Fundamentals of Qigong, Meditation, and Internal Alchemy,* vol. 1 (Valley Spirit Arts, 2013).
- *Tai Ji Jin: Discourses on Intrinsic Energies for Mastery of Self-Defense Skills,* vol. 2 (Valley Spirit Arts, 2013).
- *Tai Ji Quan: 105-Posture Yang Style Solo Form Instructions and Applications,* vol. 3 (Valley Spirit Arts, 2017).
- *Tai Ji Tui Shou: Mastering the Eight Styles and Four Skills of Sensing Hands,* vol. 4 (Valley Spirit Arts, 2014).
- *Tai Ji Bing Shu: Discourses on the Taijiquan Weapon Arts of Sword, Saber, and Staff,* vol. 6 (Valley Spirit Arts, 2014).
  Forthcoming Books in Chen Kung Series
  - *Tai Ji San Shou & Da Lu: Mastering the Two-Person Application Skills,* vol. 5.
  - *Tai Ji Wen: The Principles and Theories for Mastering Taijiquan,* vol. 7.
- *Imagination Becomes Reality: 150-Posture Taijiquan of Master T.T. Liang* (Valley Spirit Arts, 2011).
- *Steal My Art: The Life and Times of Tai Chi Master T.T. Liang* (North Atlantic Books, 2002).
- *T'ai Chi According to the I Ching—Embodying the Principles of the Book of Changes* (Healing Arts Press, 2002).
- *T'ai Chi for Kids: Move with the Animals,* illustrated by Gregory Crawford (Bear Cub Books, 2001).

- *Tai Ji Quan Treatise: Attributed to the Song Dynasty Daoist Priest Zhang Sanfeng,* Daoist Immortal Three Peaks Zhang Series (Valley Spirit Arts, 2011).
- *The Wind Sweeps Away the Plum Blossoms: Yang Style Taijiquan Staff and Spear Techniques* (Valley Spirit Arts, 2011).

Kung Fu Books
- *The Complete Guide to Northern Praying Mantis Kung Fu* (Blue Snake Books, 2010).
- *The Eighteen Lohan Skills: Traditional Shaolin Temple Kung Fu Training Methods* (Valley Spirit Arts, 2015).
- *Monk Spade: The Martial Art Weapon of Sagacious Lu* (Valley Spirit Arts, 2016).

DVDs
- **Chen Kung Series DVDs:** *Taiji Qigong, Taiji Sensing Hands,* and *Taiji Sword, Saber & Staff* (Valley Spirit Arts, 2013–15).
- *Eight Brocades Seated Qigong Exercises* (Valley Spirit Arts, 2012). Companion DVD to the book *Qigong Teachings of a Taoist Immortal.*
- *Healing Tigress Exercises* (Valley Spirit Arts, 2011).
- *Li Qingyun's Eight Brocades* (Valley Spirit Arts, 2014). Companion DVD to the book *The Immortal.*
- *Li Qingyun's Longevity Methods* (Valley Spirit Arts, 2016). Companion DVD to the book *Li Qingyun.*
- *Master T.T. Liang's 150-Posture Yang Style T'ai Chi Ch'uan Form* (Valley Spirit Arts, 1993 & 2014).
- *Master T.T. Liang Taijiquan Demonstrations* (Valley Spirit Arts, 2014).

- *Tai Ji Quan Self-Defense Instructional Program* (3-DVD Set) (Valley Spirit Arts, 2011).
- *Tiger's Waist: Daoist Qigong Restoration* (Valley Spirit Arts, 2009).
- *Wind & Dew* (Valley Spirit Arts, 2012). This version of Wind & Dew was designed to work in conjunction with the Eight Brocades DVD (also the Li Qingyun version).

Visit the Shop at Valley Spirit Arts for more information:
www.valleyspiritarts.com/shop/

About Valley Spirit Arts

Valley Spirit Arts offers books and DVDs on Taoism, Taijiquan, and meditation practices primarily from author Stuart Alve Olson, longtime student of Master T.T. Liang and translator of many Taoist related works.

Its website provides teachings on meditation and Internal Alchemy, Taijiquan, Qigong, and Kung Fu through workshops, private and group classes, and online courses and consulting.

For more information as well as updates on Stuart Alve Olson's upcoming projects and events, please visit: www.valleyspiritarts.com.

About the Sanctuary of Tao

The **Sanctuary of Tao** is a nonprofit organization dedicated to the sharing of Taoist philosophy and practices through online resources, yearly meditation retreats, and community educational programs.

The underlying mission of the **Sanctuary of Tao** is to bring greater health, longevity, and contentment to its members and everyone it serves.

Please visit www.sanctuaryoftao.org for more information about the organization and its programs.

About Liqingyun.org

Liqingyun.org is a website dedicated solely to the teachings of Li Qingyun, the 250-Year-Old Man, promoting the health and longevity practices of one of the world's oldest recorded persons.

Liqingyun.org

Li Qingyun's advice on attaining longevity and health are truly effective and practical.

Liqingyun.org features books, DVDs, raw herbs, herbal formulas, and gift items related to the teachings of Li Qingyun.

CPSIA information can be obtained
at www.ICGtesting.com
Printed in the USA
BVOW03s2143261017
498791BV00001B/10/P